The Psychiatrist who cured the Scientologist.

BY

AARON DAVID GOTTFRIED

ISBN: 978-0-9810572-0-0

Contact information: gottfriedaaron@gmail.com

Printed by: Pandora Press 33 Kent Avenue

Kitchener, Ontario N2G 3R2

All Pandora Press books are printed on Eco-Logo certified paper.

Cover design by Dan Gottfried - dang@cyberaudioonline.com

Book contents designed by Karl Griffiths-Fulton.

I would like to thank my parents William and Lois for their love and understanding through the tough and the good times.

Thank you to my Psychiatrist, Dr. M. Power, for her help and professionalism.

Thanks to Christine Horton for her help and advice.

Table of ConTenTs

DeDiCaTion

In loving memory:

to those who have lost their lives because of someone's else's cause. You are the sacrifice that continues to guide us.

ChapTer one

That week was the best week of my life. I was out of bed everyday, sometimes even before my alarm. After I pulled my sheets in what was already a glorious defeat of the upcoming day, "Magic Carpet Ride" by Steppenwolf would follow on the radio. Nothing could take away this feeling; I felt unstoppable and there was no going back to my average teenage state of mind, at least not what was average for me.

I didn't question it; I was in love, or so I thought. In combination of exercise and drinking a lot of water, I didn't question why I felt this good. I just figured it was my time: I had been in love before, but since this was stronger it was harder to identify any abnormality. It is a perfect world when one can wake up and go to bed with a smile. Most times, no one wants to question their own happiness. They just want to enjoy it.

I was told by my parents that I was sweet during this short time. I would comment on what great parents they were and are. I told them I loved them before bed every night, something I never did before and something most teenage boys don't. My mother was delighted of course, she told my father, "Oh, he's just in love." My father knew better. He didn't know what, specifically, but he knew better.

During this week or two everything between me and this girl was adorable. We would meet at the end of my street or I would walk to her house; we would go to school together, then home together. It was also her birthday during the short period of time in which we dated, which made it that much more special. It doesn't sound like much and it wasn't, but it was what I had and it felt good. My best friend had also liked this girl and they had, on at least one occasion before this point, had been seeing each other. Only in hindsight would I be able to state that I would not normally backstab a friend or so prematurely assume that I was in true love.

My 'friend-swapping' girl-friend and I spent a nice two weeks together talking, walking, hugging, and kissing. I assumed everything was going well, except for my role of having to keep the relationship secret for now, for some reason I wanted to shout out to the world that I loved this girl (even though she wasn't even my type). I wouldn't have accepted a girl that would come between friends under normal circumstances.

ChapTer Two

→

On the last day of those amazing two weeks, she walked over to my house. I assumed to spend time with me, but then the news did come. A familiar feeling I had experienced a couple times before came upon me: the feeling of all the blood in your body rushing to your heart to keep it beating, to keep it from receiving the shock to the system that it actually had just taken. The shaking from the inner most sensitive core of your body, pulsating electromagnetic currents of emotion, and the only news that makes you want to disappear to cry because the only alternative, deep down is a homicidal/suicidal rage: I was dumped. But this is giving the relationship far too much credit; in reality, we barely knew each other. As soon as I heard what was probably deep down, the inevitable because of my teenage insecurity, I felt something break.

This experience was hard on a boy who, when growing up, was unsure of himself and was also on the sensitive side. What I would feel for the next two months would seem illogical for this common teenage rite of passage. However, during this fantasy trip with this girl and while I was thrilled with the overall awe of life I had apparently caught mono. I had found this out when I ended up in the hospital due to a blood infection in my hand, which was caused by punching someone's tooth out and a student doctor at the walk-in clinic not cleaning the wound properly. I had a falling out with my friends a year or so earlier. They stole some money from me to support their new-found drug habit. I would walk by them and scowl at them on my way out to lunch everyday as they sat by the doors leading to the parking lot. Scowling was all I could do, aside from attempting to beat-up all five of them in a fit of rage to display my disgust for their disloyalty. One of their friends, a young man who I was also friends with earlier on in life, could only stand this scowling for so long.

He bolted up and yelled, "You think you're better than us?" All I could say was, "yes," because I felt that even if I had a drug habit I wouldn't steal from a friend, although I have never had a drug habit so I could've been wrong. The intense high school confrontation didn't go much further than that. Nothing much more than that was said then, until, one day when he and all my ex-buddies were waiting for me in the park. He called me, and I responded, mostly because I was walking with some girls. I walked up to him and flash-flooded him with a left then some rights. The fight ended quite quickly. I could see he didn't want to fight anymore and I didn't want to punch a face covered in blood anymore. I also had a nice gash to my left index knuckle that I wanted to take care of. The blood infection came from germs from human teeth extract situating in my blood stream too long. He lost his front tooth. I lost what would be my summer and myself.

In the hospital I watched the infection ooze out of my hand. I did not however, feel any better after the treatment. All of the sudden, I had lost my ability to see a bright side to anything and also any idea of what my inner self was, if a teenager ever did know. It was hard to feel and it seemed that there was nothing to look forward to now.

The mono, the infection, and the premature breakup all seemed to add up to a cataclysm. By this time of the year, there were assignments due in all my classes. I took the assignments home and tried to concentrate on them. I read the assignment outlines, but nothing sunk in. The words I was reading weren't making sense to me. I would just stare at the pages just looking at the words as they went out of focus, only to stare longer at the blur, then into an endless void of self-deprecating thoughts. The blur symbolized my life and where it was going.

At this point I realized I could not finish high school. The thought of attending in humiliation of my demeanor was too much to bear. Now that I thought of myself as stupid, I didn't see the point of reinforcing these feelings, which would just add to the depression. I worried about everything and I stayed away from alcohol and drugs during high school for fear that it would ruin me. This attitude faded in less than a week, and I didn't care if I finished school anymore. I didn't care whether or not if I finished the rest of my life.

What came next was a dreaded meeting with my school counselor and with my mother. She dragged me in and I didn't have the strength to put up a fight. On entering the school, I had to walk past some school acquaintances; with my mom beside me. I knew pending rumors were lurking. I didn't feel very comfortable. In addition to me and my mother, the counselor brought in a specialist, a psychologist. Far from making me feel special, it made me feel, well, fucked up enough to need a specialist. I was now officially a difficult case and it only took a week or so to get this way.

"How are you today Aaron?" she asked.

"Not good." I couldn't look anyone in the eyes. My stare fixated on a specific fiber of the carpet.

"What's been happening lately?" "What's wrong?"

"I don't know," I said and then looked up at her honestly, straight in the eyes and told her that I wanted to die. To avoid that common response of, "oh no you don't, c'mon now," I said it and she knew it, and there was really nothing left to say. I take it that I sounded and looked convinced against any attempt of therapy, since there was none that followed. Though, maybe I could have used some consoling.

For the first time, I said out loud that I wanted to die, and that there was no reason for me to go on living. Discussing this topic in the same career counselor's room that I previously had serious conversations regarding my future was a disappointment to my counselor, to say the least: she started to sob. This made me want God to come right then and there and rip my heart out and send me deep into hell. At least in hell you belong with all the others. How long could I be amongst people who wanted to live?

The specialist had hardly said a word. He looked at me with those 'son, good luck,' eyes. The young can only assume what a person is thinking when they're saying nothing. The school psychologist had a few words with me and I wasn't very responsive. My counselor tried to suck back her tears, but she wasn't doing a very good job. I didn't blame her though. This only showed she cared for me as she did for all of her students. She couldn't fathom how a bright boy, who had everything going for him, so they say, could drastically change like this. Nor did anyone else understand, for that matter. The psychologist told my mother that she needed to get some help for me, meaning a psychiatrist. They suggested that I try to attend a couple classes or even one day starting the following Monday to see how I'd feel, then take it from there.

My mother and I walked out of there shortly after we walked in. We went home and I felt the kind of anxiety that wasn't believable. My cousins had come over to visit that day and I couldn't even speak to them. My eyes glazed over with a type of psychotic notion, a type of mental attempt to numb all feeling, a defense mechanism to void it out like a heroin junkie on a high.

The weekend passed and on Monday I tried to attend some classes. I heard whispers around me in class making me cringe. I walked home like a zombie on that very vibrant day. I wasn't even aware that I was walking, but aware that I had to get home fast enough so no fellow students could converse with me. The embarrassment was unreal; I went from a basketball player with good grades, to a pathetic sight as this was baffling. Accompanying this embarrassment was total disinterest in what anyone else thought of me. I was embarrassed because this wasn't like me, but I couldn't feel any other way. I could only feel my anxiety and numbness inside. I just wanted to be away from prying eyes; I managed to escape these eyes of judgment by leaving school; I could not deal with school anymore and I did not go, so I was given my credits with the help of my counselor. This would enable me to start fresh next year and put all of this behind me. I knew, however that I would not be around come next fall.

ChapTer Three

At this time, I started to pretty much spend my living existence in bed. When a mind is riddled with anxiety to an extreme degree, it gets to the point where it physically hurts to move. I knew what I was feeling was not normal. But how often do we question our own state of mind? We just feel it and react to it: I acted no differently. I accepted this state of being, as if I didn't know I had any other choice. It was physically, mentally, emotionally and spiritually impossible for me to think a positive thought. My brain would not let any serotonin in or any spark of anything stimulating into my concept. The spring of 1997 was blossoming and so was I, at least that's what I had thought. I embraced the way I felt then because there was no feeling any other way and now there was no getting around this pounding throb of infinite dread.

This dread didn't pass with the onset of that girl returning to see me every so often. I wouldn't come out to see her, but she would talk to my mother about me. They would talk about how I was and how I was feeling. How she really did like me but, blah, blah, blah. It didn't matter anymore to me. Obviously this wasn't all about her; I had much deeper problems to think about and think about, analyze, and reanalyze. She was the trigger and the infection was the climax of something else, maybe. I didn't care about anyone that might care about me because my life as I knew it would be over. Soon, I hoped.

How can a dream become death?
We think death is rest. A fantasy of an
execution. Brightened by lightening.
Everything anybody wants.
No matter how disheartening.
Is only what we think,
Is the best for us at the time.

Every night I had aches and pains which was followed by anxiety about the present, about the future, or about whatever. The anxiety that would normally keep someone awake was outweighed by a tremendous need to escape from reality. I was never a substance user and getting drugs would take some effort. This anxiety never kept me awake because I slept to escape. My sleep was my only salvation. Nightmares were my reality with every waking second; they were not in my dreams. It's amazing how much one can sleep with some determination.

My parents tried to be supportive. They understood that something was wrong and they told me that they would try to get me help if this didn't pass. My mother would talk to me everyday and try to shed some light on the situation. She had experienced depression before and had some idea of what I was going through. They asked questions like, 'why did I feel this bad? and 'how did it happen so quickly?' They knew in their hearts that there was a reason for this, and it was something beyond what I or they could see. It didn't seem rational to them that I could have been faking this depression to get attention. That just wasn't like me. I didn't fit the profile and I had no reason to stir this up. This depression wasn't normal either, considering what had happened being fairly minuscule. There had to be some underlying cause, something that would explain this pain. However, the answer would not be necessarily easy to swallow. My parents would stop at nothing to find out what was going on. I was lucky because of this, but I didn't the time to wait for the answer.

My mother would come and talk to me each day to try to get me out of my numbing slumber. The conversations would usually go something like this:

"Hi, Aaron? How are you feeling?"

I normally wouldn't really respond, just barely look her in the eyes and giving a pathetic frown, indicating how I felt.

"Hmm? How do you feel? She would ask again. "Not very good." I moaned.

"Oh, how did you sleep?" "Ok."

Her real reason for checking on me wasn't to see if I was feeling okay; it was to make sure I was alive. Understandably, if your son says he wants to die what kind of parents sit back and call his bluff.

"Are you having bad thoughts still?"

"Yes." And this seemed to be the answer for longer than was bearable.

A suicidal person can get to the point where they want to kill themselves just out of embarrassment. He may not actually be ready to do it, but it is jump-started by his realization that he is

10

causing strain on everybody. I wasn't the kind of person to accept being embarrassed.

"What are you thinking?"

"That I feel like dying." I would always underplay it by using words like 'feel' and 'want,' instead of 'are' and 'will.' I didn't want to upset her too much.

"Have you heard the saying, 'this too shall pass?' " "Yes."

"It will you know. Nothing stays constant in this universe. Everything changes. You won't feel like this forever. You just have to hold on and try to overcome this."

"But I don't feel like its going away." I thought it was getting worse.

"You have to trust me. You remember when I was sick when you were younger? (my mother had coming and going trials with MS). I was so sick and I couldn't move. I wanted to die everyday. I would pray to God every night that he just take me. But you know, I'm glad he didn't because things started to get better. Things will for you too."

It sounded fair enough, and it was something that could lift my spirits a little. Then my mind would think well, she couldn't kill herself, she had a family to live for, and she had kids who needed her. Even if she wanted to kill herself, she had no excuse to do so. People depended on her. What and who did I have, really? This was my twisted rationalization that started to sink in. The anxiety and fear was so much that my mother would have to lift me out of bed so I could wash myself some days.

What did I have going for me now? Everyone who did love me was being brought down by me. I wasn't in school and didn't plan on going back. I didn't have a job and couldn't have

11

one in my current state. My friends couldn't be bothered with this, and I wouldn't let them be. In less than two weeks, I made myself inconsequential to the world.

It's very possible to trick your mind into believing no one will miss you in order to serve your selfish needs. Human beings do this all the time; we choose to see the angles we want and deny the ones that will cause us guilt or pain. Because we are all in need of momentary pleasure, we think we're pulling a little white lie over the heads of people we care about, when in actuality, we are only tricking ourselves.

A couple more days passed and the need for the deed grew inside me. I didn't think about anyone else anymore. I didn't think about how my mom would feel if I were gone. Not that I didn't care, it just ceased to cross my mind. Dying became a constant in my psyche, drawing more power every hour. This addiction of thought soon became fixed until my brain cells began to die. My fix would become a permanent one and I wasn't afraid to check out anymore. Anyway you want to look at it, this was my temporary solution; temporary because I knew that this isn't a long term solution. I had been taught and knew through belief in my heart that our lives don't end when our bodies die. So what did this mean in my realm of belief? It meant I could be stuck somewhere in a haze of spiritual bafflement until I was sorted out by the law enforcement above. Alternatively, I could be stuck on earth just hanging around people that gave me warmth for awhile. Another possibility is that I could find another womb, embody it and possibly go through this same problem again at the age of 17, only so God or whoever could test me again. Believing this, I still wanted to blow my fucking brains out my ear.

The answer was meaningless because it was nowhere to be found. It would not come into focus for some time. Until then, I had no real rational reason or excuse for my emotional overtones, which is what sent me so deep, so quickly. There was no humiliation this conceivably bad, I thought. It's funny, in a non-humorous way, how nothing in reality is as good as our dreams, but everything can get worse than our nightmares. The itch was about to reach a climax.

ChapTer four

From what I heard it wasn't the easiest or most effective way to get the job done. Furthermore, I wasn't feeling social enough or motivated enough to go out and find a gun. I knew from stories how often alcohol and pills fail. I was never one for heights and worried that I might survive the jump. I had been wanting to do this for what seemed like an eternity (only two weeks actually) but I just woke up from sleep at 3 a.m. and decided this was it. Anxiety becomes like an excruciating pain both mentally and physically when it stresses the mind enough.

I was looking at my kung-fu belts I had received years earlier and thought they might be good for a hanging. Then I saw some shoe laces on my dresser and made what looked to be something I didn't learn in the boy scouts. Whatever little knot I made, I tied around my closet pole for clothes and wrapped the laces around my neck pretty tight. It seemed as though this might do the trick. In my mind I hoped it would, although I'm sure that somewhere in my unconscious I still had a flicker of life. Nonetheless, I lifted my legs up and let the rain pour down.

I was surprised at my determination. This wasn't an orthodox hanging of course. But this way I had to fight to keep it up. It was painful until my legs started twitching and convulsing. My legs kicked and ironically broke the little man on my favourite kung-fu trophy. He symbolized me as triumphant at one point in my life, therefore breaking him at this juncture in my life was incredibly symbolic. I remember the day I won that trophy and how proud I was to make my father so happy. This was one of my few glorious moments as a child. I felt like I was still a child now, but with nothing to hold on to. I kept clenching and keeping my legs up with my arms with the laces tightening around my neck, and the blood was rushing very quickly to my head, so I couldn't lay my feet on the ground and stand. This is what I was sure I had wanted and before I could question myself, I was gone. Only black surrounded my world as it had previously, but without thought. Like a dreamless sleep, something I would've taken any day or night of the week to escape my consuming thoughts.

I don't know how long I was out for. I assume it was until the sheer pain around my neck kicked in, knocking me into consciousness. I tore the laces from around my neck and head and crashed to the floor, gasping for breath. Flashes of thought came in between deep, hard breaths of how stupid that was. How stupid that was, I thought. But in a strange way, I also forgave myself because the agony of life was so great. If anyone felt the way I did, I was convinced, they would surely seek refuge in a similar way.

I gasped and cried. But I was still lifeless. I could put no energy forth, I could only sob. But I stopped from this as soon as I could because this was no time to cry and feel this pain. It was time to sleep more and escape this feeling for at least the next few hours. I crawled along the floor to my bed still trying to breath, calmed myself and somehow fell asleep fairly quickly in my mental desperation for rest.

You would think it would be hard to sleep after passing out from strangulation, and you would be right if I was actually suicidal under my own volition and behavior. I had to forget rather than confront what I had just done. I did what I had been doing for a few weeks; I was used to shutting down my mind of thought. Focusing on the sweet nothingness of sleep was motivation enough for my body to soothe itself and give up energy. All would be fine until the next day, but I didn't have to deal with the next day until it came.

My mother was making her usual daily morning rounds the next day to check if I was okay, dead or still there. She sat at my bedside and asked how I was doing. I was non-responsive as usual to indicate that I was not really well. She sort of pulled down the sheet as I was covering my neck with it. Again, I didn't really respond except for a look of fear and utter shame. I always pretended to be asleep to avoid conversation, until she woke me up, which was fair considering it was mid-afternoon. I thought there might have been a mark left behind from the incident the night before, although I was hoping of course that there wouldn't be. She sensed something though, as some mothers do, whether it was something in me or possibly seeing some commotion around my closet area. She eventually got me to bring down the covers to reveal a reddish scarring encircling around my neck. She gasped when she saw the sickening sight before her. Even though she expected something like this to happen, actually witnessing the evidence was an unbelievable event for her. I grasped at the sheets and pulled back up to my neck. After this, we didn't own our lives anymore.

How do you explain to a mother (a good one at that) who has done her best to raise you, why you want to end your life? The shame is too great to harvest words and no words will suffice the pain. I sank lower into my pillow and at that moment I would have been happier if I were the mattress so she couldn't see my face. However my despair was so high and my tone was so low that I couldn't actually muster shame toward her because that would entail me caring what she thought. I was in such a state of apathy and at that point I didn't care what others thought because my need to die heightened and brought on more selfish ideas. Normally, I definitely would've cried in that moment. But of course crying is a healthy thing and I was something indescribable and definitely not that. My tears were spent and my fear was so overwhelming it was hard to cry; I was just completely quite numb.

Terrified of what someone might see.
Always being, what we are afraid to look at.
All absolutes in this world Seem to have some
contradictions.
Are we meant to understand anything?
I now cope with all afflictions.
I recognize all addiction. I understand
nothing.
We all long for something That doesn't even
exist.

She took the suicide attempt as any good mother would, and that was badly. There was no demeaning or verbal punishment. She didn't freak out or get hysterical; she was probably expecting that I would eventually try something, but just hoped it wouldn't be that. After her gasp subsided she sat there with me, wondering what to do next. There wasn't much to ask me. She couldn't ask why, because she knew why. Her mind was

17

definitely racing at this point; however, she had to do something quick. If I could've spoke, I wouldn't have told her that I wouldn't try anything like this again just to calm her nerves. I could not guarantee it. I really didn't want to cause her pain; I just wanted to end my own, although telling her this might not have been truthful because I didn't know when the pain would end or if it ever would. I didn't know when I would be myself again.

I wanted to say how sorry I was, but I've always been quite selfish. I wasn't worried about anyone else because I was directly afflicted and consumed by this sickness. Also, I wasn't capable of empathy since I was feeling so sympathetic towards myself. I would describe myself more as apathetic, since this degree of sympathy would require a reason. I wanted to say, 'I'm sorry Mommy, I know this isn't right and I can do better.' But I wasn't in control of my emotions. People aren't always in control of themselves or their future. It wasn't me that hanged myself, it was a zombie version of my altered state.

It's interesting to wonder why I didn't die, whether it was luck, my own unconscious fighting will, or simply not enough pressure put on my neck. What is fascinating is the predicaments people put themselves in, and their outcomes and the reasons for these outcomes. Fate, will, luck, conscious and unconscious drives, and karma are all what we might consider reasons for things that happen, but to consider all of these at once creates confusion. To lessen this confusion in varying degrees, we instead generalize and say everything happens for a reason. It's just funny that no one ever wonders if it's a good reason. I suppose it's implied, but not always true at all. It was not my time to die that night. I am not saying this wasn't good in the long run of course, but after attempting this and surviving it made me see how numbingly alive I still was. It always seems better to be dead than be completely void of emotion. The point of living is not to be alive, but to feel alive.

My mother became increasingly panicked. The threat of suicide was not taken lightly up until now, but this couldn't go on any longer. I could hear her upstairs phoning people in desperation for some help. She called my best friend to come over and talk with me that day. I didn't want my best friend to see me in this compromising, pathetic state but I hadn't wanted to see anyone in weeks anyway and he was on his way regardless. The panic of someone with the ability to spread the word of my state was scary. My mind was warping into ways of thinking that had no logic or sanity. Then again, in my experience you can't really trust anyone in high school anyway. But to escape or to say anything different was impossible because I was speechless with my discontent.

When he arrived we sat at the end of my bed together uncomfortable and awkward. He attempted to make small talk. However, I wasn't feeling chatty, to say the least. He asked me a few questions and made some light comments to which my responses to both were "ya" or "I dunno:" basically grunts along with a shoulder shrugs. He brought up reassuringly that basketball season would be up and running and we need to start practicing because the team needed me. It felt good, but how could I think about basketball when it made me sick to walk. How could I be this ill? Before I wanted to die, but now I felt that I deserved to die. No one can be this pathetic and deserve to live. How could I justify to my best friend, a guy with whom I was always in competition and who was like a brother to me, that I wanted to tap out for good? The vulnerability ate me up and I hung my head and he left. I didn't mind.

19

ChapTer five

I would not be able to remain in the sanctity of my room away from peering eyes forever. This attempt on my life meant something had to be done, and now. No one trusted me not to risk my life again and sadly I couldn't give anyone any assurance myself. Therefore, I found myself in a car on the way to the hospital. Surprisingly I didn't put up a fight against those judging eyes; I was still passive, and for some strange reason I've never felt safer anywhere than in a hospital aside from home. I've never been a hypochondriac, and although school seemed socially unbearable for me, the hospital provided a break from this and seemed safe. I did want the safety which I couldn't trust within myself and I knew I needed help. I was just too fucked up to give a shit whether I got it or not. I just wanted to get better or die, not sit in this ultimate funk forever.

I don't remember entering the hospital, but I remember being placed a gurney and rolled onto the elevator. Before going down, a nurse came into focus when she approached me and my mother. I recognized her as a friend of my mothers. When I was younger we went on road trips with her and her kids, and I always had a crush on her daughter. She said a few words to my mother before looking at me and said "Aaron... How could you do this? What's going on? Why would you want to do this?"

I looked in her eyes for a short time, and then turned my head. I couldn't face this and I was gone. How could she question me when she didn't know what was going on? In my irrational brain chemistry at the time I thought she had no right to ask me this. It was none of her business. Looking back at it now she had every right to ask this, but it wouldn't be until later that I would realize she actually didn't understand what many health practitioners didn't understand at this time. I'm not talking about being another pathetic teenager who felt sorry for himself, but whatever was wrong was not complicated but apparently not easily detectable.

She didn't stay around long because she was working. The elevator went down a floor and in no time I was on my way to the psychiatric ward. I always believed that the psychotics belonged here. Ending up here could've made me think that anyone could wind up here, but it pretty much reaffirmed my idea that I'm going crazy or that I obviously already was. This did not initially help the recovery process.

Sitting on the end of my new bed and holding a pill in my hand felt unreal to me. I was sitting and staring at it in a dream-like state, not knowing whether to take it or not, just as my dad entered into the room after pacing around outside in a nervous mess. This pill symbolized a defeat of a dream in the palm of my hand: the dream of being both a son and a productive man for his parents. I knew little of my parents' religious beliefs, but I knew this pill was against theirs. If I took it and went to sleep in a Psych Ward everything would be over, even though people around me were telling me that it was okay to take it, and so I did, because it wasn't as if it didn't seem over already. I looked up in my parents' eyes to verify that this was the correct choice, and they told me to go ahead. At this point, it did not seem as though there was another choice.

As the night came, the darkness stayed. I lay in my bed, pretending to be asleep, but I actually couldn't sleep because of the medication. My mother stayed late and watched me. I faked sleep as she sat there crying and sobbing. I probably could've said something but her crying almost annoyed me. This was my problem I thought and something I couldn't help. Something was overtaking me, something seemingly evil. For all I knew it was myself now. I would later realize that when the human being feeds the idea to give up and give in is the true and only evil that really exists. I couldn't even muster the words to say that I was sorry. I listened to her bawl on what happened to be Mother's Day, while I was not aware and totally void of emotion. Being too consumed with myself to even know what day it was, I lay there as the nurses came in and consoled her. Something I couldn't do for what I was doing to her.

I was put on the anti-depressant Paxil. It started to make my mood better quite quickly. Over a ten day stay at the hospital I was out and feeling better. This wouldn't last very long and neither would my relationship with Paxil. I was feeling better with the pill, but I was taken off it around the time I was released from hospital. My father, persuaded by his belief in Scientology, demanded that I be taken off Paxil because it was against his religious beliefs. As a result, within a two week period I went from a psychotic severe depression, to becoming a little better and actually seeing friends, and finally into a comatose normal depression that would last the rest of the summer. It would turn out an anti-depressant wasn't what I needed anyway.

In search of assistance, as well as to report their ethical mistake in parenting with medication, my father reported our dilemma to a bigger Church of Scientology than our own mission. It was kind of like admitting your sins. Even after I was off the anti- depressant, my mother received phone calls insulting her and accusing her of child abuse because they were supposed to know better, as they were quite high up in Scientology. As if anyone else knew what we were going through. As if I could've actually gotten worse on medication than I had already been. There was no worse. The fear Scientology has of medication is that it numbs the senses and makes people into zombies. Also, the church is worried that the medication will produce addictive personality traits towards drugs and when taken off will affect people heavily producing symptoms of withdrawal. The general theory is that all psychiatrists are still trying to lobotomize everyone, which I'm not sure was ever the case in general. The point is I was a threat to myself already and I've met several junkies and zombies that weren't.

My parents were torn between their sanity and mine and torn between what was best for me and what the church said was best for me. No one knew because it was not known what was going on. I suppose the hope was that this would pass and that I would turn back into the motivated young man I used to be.

The summer had to go on whether or not I wanted to be a part of it. As it lagged on, the phone calls from the church kept coming. They told my mother to do this and that and what they thought was right. My father was the main incentive of importance being higher up the ladder in Scientology and having money, which seemed to be a reason to keep on their lines frequently.

The rest of the summer consisted of more of the same. I was usually in my bed or watching television, basically. What would occasionally give me a twinkle in my step would be if my parents would leave and I'd go to the kitchen and gorge on whatever food to feel some comfort. I understood obesity after a few weeks. When you have nothing food isn't a bad friend, very fleeting but at the ripe age of 18 everything I ever had seem to leave anyway. There was always more food.

Some nights I would steal my dad's BMW and go out for a joy ride. I would normally be quite panicky about driving with no license, but I felt I needed some stimulation due to the lack of it in these last months. I'd been feeling dead or next to it for some time, but you can't help but feel somewhat alive going 100 mph listening to "Welcome to the Jungle." Of course the idea crossed my mind to drive that car straight into a fucking cement block. That however would've been gory and if it failed I would be more suicidal than even before, laid out in a hospital bed. Ultimately, I didn't have the courage and why ruin a beautiful expensive automobile to end my worthless life.

As the summer ended, my tone went up a little. At least on the Scientology tone scale it did, from apathy to angry. I'm not belittling this idea, I agree that this is a progression, but this was scary. Before I was sick emotionally, but now I felt sick in the head and unable to identify what was happening. I found myself with a bag and putting a fake gun inside.

Part of me was possibly thinking that if I couldn't kill myself maybe someone else could. When a person leaves their mind, the body is controlled by something else.

So I waited until my parents went to bed until I got on my black clothes. Thinking back now, I don't know why I wore black. It fit the mood and I was hiding something, a feeling, a motive. Maybe subconsciously I wanted to be caught for something and locked up so I wouldn't hurt myself.

It felt apparent that I had turned from a literally innocent teenager to something demented, a tortured being. As the sleek truck drove straight my eyes scanned the sidewalks watching people who had purpose.

Just before turning off the main street on my way home I pulled behind a police cruiser. After staring at the cruiser for awhile, I followed it from close behind for some time down main street and down some streets. I fantasized about them getting a stolen car call and pulling me over. I would get out and pull the fake hand gun and it would all be over finally, not my life but this pain.

The cops turned off and my heart felt human with rational fear for the first time in awhile I felt a little human. You can't suddenly lose your conscience unless you lose your mind and that hadn't happened yet. I drove home and decided to try to put this behind me.

Coming home I pulled up to my block. Our neighborhood block was so small and open that I could see my backyard from the other street. I could see that the light was on in the kitchen. The bashing lecture which I was sure to come home to was surprisingly disappointing and very opposite to what I expected. It was disappointing because when parents won't even waste their breath anymore, you know they've given up on you. As I came in the back door all I received was a let down tired gaze in their eyes followed by "Give me the keys" and then

"Go to bed." This was done without a fight, just as complacent and pathetic as the night had begun.

To look through the eyes of someone else, To be someone other then yourself.
The most unfortunate day, To have ever graced ones stay.
On this whirlwind that only few spin through.

ChapTer Six

After getting caught, the grand theft auto slowed down for awhile. I spent the rest of the summer in bed or watching television or going to doctors to find out what was wrong with me physically or mentally or both. I went to specialists for blood work and tests. I even went to a neurologist to have tests and an M.R.I. After words he sat my mother and I down and explained simply that it was his expert opinion that this dilemma was behavioral, meaning there was no internal or external force causing my irrationality. (He decided to only test me for M.S) I was basically just suddenly a burden on society and this was my fault. My mother was neither impressed nor convinced by this conclusion. As we left and crossed the road she screamed my name out as I took a step forward into oncoming traffic, thinking I was walking into it purposely. This was not the plan; I was just getting ready to cross the street. I was however thinking about it after her assumption. For her to think that I was purposely walking into traffic didn't make the day any better, although I couldn't blame her. Her nerves were shot and I was beyond feeling mine.

Aside from having doctor's appointments throughout the summer, the rest of it was spent in the basement in solitude, just waiting out my bout. Not sure if it would pass, but at least hoping it would which was hope for the future. This was an improvement from the absolute grimness I had felt before. If I did go out I would see all the pretty girls in their summer clothes and it started to come into focus that with all the terror in this world, the pretty girls that were around was something to live for. This didn't quite end the depression yet.

I learned many things that would allow me to empathize with humankind during this time, things that would allow me to have supporting conversations with people in the future. At this point I could already relate with others with depression and suicide. I could relate to an obese person. When I wasn't hiding or sobbing in the basement I was sneaking food from upstairs. It was comfort in replacement for having nothing else. Maybe it's not complicated at all and easy to understand but, going through a time, even it being short, can cause a realization for a more important understanding.

Experiencing a serious depression over only the course of two months has enabled me to understand depression in general. I had gone through all possible stages in three months. When none of your friends have ever been through anything, you start to feel like an outcast. But later on I would meet people that I could talk to and understand. In later life, you see how the harshness in this world can make your existence more livable in the long run. You can't learn anything fully without experiencing it firsthand: what we read and what we hear will always be secondhand knowledge and always possibly unreal. It is only what we know, which is knowledge, and we only know what is our own.

Stepping briefly behind the eyes of the irreversibly violent I could take with me a pity for this kind of person walking mine or your street. Not to accept, but to have a general understanding of not the actions but what lead to them, because you cannot explain what isn't rationally human. Make no mistake; there is no empathy or sympathy because we all of course have a choice to make in life before every partaking. But I had a sort of crash course in what would normally be years of degradation, abuse, misguidance, and self loathing to get to that point. I wasn't ready to hurt anyone, but I touched an area in my brain that entertained the idea and realized what it took to get to this point, also realizing that this place is conceivable for anyone to reach. This void of emotion I would come to know as a negligence of self and self love, a point where no love is let in anymore and all attempts to enjoy life through these means have been sabotaged. After words, I did not see a reason to know these things, but instead a reason to know how to stop these things from happening.

I did not know what was going to happen or what to do. I remained fairly docile until the end of the summer. Watching the idiot box one night did actually have an effect on how I felt. As I said, I had lost confidence in all aspects of what a young man needs, and an important part of that was my intellect. I had convinced myself that I was stupid, and when you are young and stupid you relay all judgment of intelligence towards academics in school.

So as I began, I was watching T.V. one night and the advertisement for Mega Memory comes on. I'm sure most of you can remember - they're going on about all this crap you can remember, and saying high school has nothing to do with intelligence anyway, that it's just memory work. Some have it some don't. I knew this deep down, but I felt that this was my way to feel smart again. If this was for real I could go back to school and get straight A's and everything would be fine, although getting good grades in school was never a problem for me. However I jumped up with a tenacity like I used to after too much sugar and a Jean Claude Van Damme movie as a kid. I felt better now. It was that easy and that fast. A silly fucking trigger.

It seems ludicrous, that an infomercial would get me in high spirits; nonetheless I was jumping for joy, literally. I went to bed that night with a smile on my face for the first time in two and half months. The next day I told my mom to order the Mega Memory Kit for me, which she did. It wasn't long after that when I informed my parents that I wanted to go back to school. About two weeks into the next year. This one and only stupid thing brought me out of my deep depression which in turn would be the real thing that questioned my sanity or the believability of my affliction. I needed something to spark an interest back into the game of life and if it was this I wasn't going to complain. It felt good to feel good again. In fact it felt great, as not only was I going to enjoy it but I was going to make it my business to only feel great from now on and to never feel that sickness again.

ChapTer Seven

Returning to school late still seemed like a feat that would be better left unfulfilled, however I could hardly sit around the house for the rest of my life especially since I was feeling better. I had to not only enter school two weeks late, which might cause some talk amongst fellow classmates, but I assumed there was still a bit of a buzz about me leaving early last year. I was never one to give a shit what people thought and that's what bothered me so much, the fact that I cared so much about what they thought at this point, but high school was insidious. The lower your confidence is, the more you care about others opinions about your person; this is simply because you don't respect your own opinion, so in turn you seek approval.

Whether a person's confidence was high or low, I've never understood nor trusted anyone who has described high school as a tolerable, or even worse, as an enjoyable experience. I had a fairly non-humiliating high school experience. To be in a building with a thousand plus people who are all different and expect things to coincide splendidly is ridiculous. This is obvious. High school is where we can build strengths and learn to survive social hardships. It's just troubling that we have to do it this way where the halls are filled with judging eyes and people who pry into the lives of others. Anyone who liked or got along with most people were either too scared to say what they meant or were so desperate for popularity and acceptance that they gave up a part of themselves. I suppose maybe we don't always know ourselves and maybe I would've had a better time if I was even nicer than I tried to be. It just didn't seem real. I didn't want to know an adolescent who didn't judge, or anyone who was a prep hiding behind an opinion-less face - whether or not they were aware of it. I never believed anyone could have anymore than five close friends; it seems statistically improbable unless you're a droid. School does prepare us for work, but not in an education sense, no not at all. It prepares us for having to share space with people we dislike and unconsciously prepare us to keep a straight face. This is how it seemed anyway, but each day was getting more blurry.

The first week or so back I kept it quite hush hush. I attended classes and just hoped no one knew how I was the previous summer. No kid wants to be the subject of ridicule or rumour and this time was no different personally. It's a mind tearing experience being a self conscious teenager and not knowing if someone is looking at you - for a reason or for no reason at all. I knew what those troubled kids felt like in this instant. A summer's worth of hardship and now I felt like "one of those kids." To be in a box and be labeled is to be young. I felt like a certain type now, which has no reality as an adult. Not because it stops, but because later in life we can surround ourselves with people that would never judge us. It was an eye opening experience to walk in about 3 different pairs of shoes in 3 months, I felt like I understood people a little more now. This acceptance was something I learned, but I wouldn't learn how to practice it for quite some time. Before full-maturity and full-confidence to which all of us do not ever attain judgment of others will always be our main form of fleeting self-fulfillment. This is a true testament of our lack of growth and evolution.

I remember one day this week, I was passing through the halls and I was stopped by two people who hardly knew me. I supposed they felt they knew me well enough or that we were even friends, because they asked me if it was true that I had been on anti depressants last summer (Back in 1998 I suppose this was a big deal, but only five years later one of every three teenagers would be introduced to medication of some kind). I was not yet at the emotional ability of boldness to show any kind of resentment towards their blatant rudeness. I just answered a few of their questions and tried to make light of the situation, even though I was quite embarrassed. When the slew of questioning was done, I left.

Everyday I started to talk to fellow classmates more and more, and eventually warmed back up to the school experience. My vacation was only as long as the summer basically, but I felt as though there had been somewhere from which I could never quite return. The experience didn't change me, instead it changed my view of what could happen and nothing could ever be worse than that feeling. Nothing in me would let that feeling happen again. I wanted to experience the best in life now. I felt exhilarated that I wasn't dead and I could feel every air molecule making up my breath making me feel alive, and more alive than I ever was before.

Over time, the comfort that I was beginning to feel became confidence. I enjoyed this confidence and what better way to build confidence than to do something that you're good at. So, I began playing basketball again. Tryouts were coming up and I had to be in tip-top shape. I felt I had to go to the other extreme to get as far away from the past as possible, so this confidence would soon become an ego. Even false confidence feels better than self ridicule. What made me feel like a real person again was basketball. I played harder than ever before and I was working out more than ever. I was becoming strong and my energy was abundant. This new-found energy and understanding for life would soon isolate me at the other side of the border; not from embarrassment, but egotism. I remember thinking that I was better, but not knowing the reason. It was real to me and I wasn't faking, just acting out the other side of the spectrum, since it was much more pleasing. Maybe I felt I was someone special for getting over a teenage crisis or that I had a revelation. Or maybe I was angry that it happened and still had blame. Maybe I could be stronger on my own. I just knew I couldn't be scared anymore and I couldn't hold on to my personality without changing it. Thus, every game on the court became a battle and it became violent. Every game with a friend got ugly and trash talking got personal. A little bit of me died that summer and this alter ego was fun. He didn't take shit and had the balls to say whatever he wanted. I wasn't that sweet kid anymore, but that never seemed to get me anywhere before anyway. At least this way I was reciprocating some of the pain I went through, outwardly. After a crisis you must get through the sadness, and then face the anger. The anger always feels better because we project it upon external factors. The sadness involves blaming inwardly: a person can only blame self so much before an emotional collapse and that pain ends up being directed elsewhere.

That part of my life was over. There was no worry about much anymore. As worried about grades as I used to be, I began to not worry about them at all, as I assumed that things would work themselves out. I was intelligent I didn't need a piece of paper to prove that. As I thought more, I came to the conclusion that school was a joke and any teacher worth mentioning in my school still didn't have a clue or the IQ for that matter to match my wit, so why try for them? Everything seemingly was going to be fine. I was sick, and now I was ok; I was sad, and now I was happy. I was starting to think a lot about things I could do and things I had to do, so much so that I was beginning to lose sleep at night, but I thought that this was all part and parcel with a productive life. I had reason to live now, so why waste time with sleep. I started to adopt a personal policy that sleep was for the weak. It wouldn't be long until I would have personal challenges with my mind and body to see how long I could stay awake and how much I could do in a day.

This energy didn't really subside, it just seemed to grow. I would get tired here and there, but sleep time turned into more of a nap/pass out period, for an hour or two. In that fall I remember biking to my best friends house after walking and biking all morning and having not slept the night before or that week for that matter. I knocked on his door to see that he wasn't home. I kind of wanted to see him and waited on the lawn for a bit, I then just went to sleep all sprawled out on his front lawn beside my bike. My mother heard about this later, so I assumed that my friend came home with his mom and they left again feeling uncomfortable that I was there. This didn't seem strange to me.

On weekends, I spent time at the universities in town playing older players or other players from the high schools. I would usually get in a pushing match with someone or a whole group of guys. It didn't matter to me. I would do this on weekends, only to come back to high school and start fights with my teammates. I didn't seem to care anymore; I wanted the ball and I wanted to embarrass my own teammates so I could prove something. Coaches thought at first I was on steroids because of a massive attitude and some mass added to my body from lifting weights a 3 a.m. I had never played with such energy as I had in those few months. Not just energy, but an over–aggressive attitude as well. I remember practices when I rejected shots down teammate's throats with physical and vocal authority and a game when I fouled out before half time. However, I felt that the coach was an idiot for not pulling me sooner. There was a justification for every action.

Right or wrong, this didn't seem to pierce my psyche. I can't remember if I had the sense to tell the difference between them. No, I was not myself but who was I? I was still a teenager and my make up hadn't been fully generated; who was I to say that I knew who I was when I didn't? This attitude didn't feel so much right as it felt good. This false confidence was serving a need to not be scared of life or people anymore. As time passed, it felt like this was it, there was no other way to feel. I was on a constant high, something the burnouts could never buy. This was who I was meant to be. If no one else could match my energy why was I in trouble if not spectacular.

Hatred underneath, for people's strengths.
A jealousy for something you don't know
exists. You can't see in yourself the good
that others do, And won't accept an
opinion they have of you.
Torn between a negative and a negative view,
Only to end up alone, praying for a positive
in solitude.

I found out later that during parent teacher interviews with my parents my English teacher had a clue to my behaviour that could have possibly helped us. She sat down with my parents and, after a discussion about my ignorant behavior, she asked if I was Bipolar. My parents said no, because I had never had any mental problems before this summer. I hadn't been diagnosed with anything. She must have known a little about the condition and thought that I displayed some of the symptoms. She said I'd walk in the class like I owned it. However, this theory was soon thrown out; possibly my parents took some offense to it, but they still took note of the suggestion. They considered my actions a teenage phase that I would grow out of. I was just having some problems adapting to puberty, it will work itself out. This teacher, although rather bitchy in the classroom, displayed a keen sense of awareness at this point that should have been jumped on or even discussed further at this meeting. This was a surprising observation, but as some teachers tend to do, it was given out as more of a judgment than an educational guess or possibly life saving suggestion, and therefore it was thrown out.

The Canadian fall with its magnificence carried me a little further. The air and wind was my breath giving me all the energy I needed to carry on and on with no sleep and I did so ever cherish in my younger days. I had become more confident in my abilities as a person and my arrogance seemed to leave me more alone. I preferred to be alone, but when I did want company I found I had none because I had alienated my friends with my insults. Normally they would have told me to fuck off, but I was starting to scare people. During this period of no sleep my eyes had a permanent glaze over and my pupils had dilated some. I started to look intimidating and somewhat insane and for awhile they did become eyes of hate. Everyone walking by was an enemy and it seemed like me against the world. My friends appeared to be gone and I hated my basketball team. I shrugged this off and anything else at this time because who needed them. I felt they couldn't make me better because I thought I was the best, so why bother playing with them, I thought. I couldn't figure out if I had hurt my best friend or if he was ashamed of me. I would say so much sometimes and not even remember what I said, and even if I did, I was too stubborn to apologize. It was possible that I didn't fit the image he was always trying desperately to convey. In the confusion I would just say to hell with them. So I said to hell with all of it.

The decision was to quit school. I felt school was holding me back. What was it holding be back from? Well I had a lot of egotistical ideas at the time and I felt as though I could do anything. Of course we're all capable of basically anything, but I knew in my mind that all of these things I could do without any previous experience. I believed that I was so talented in whatever I chose to do that I didn't need an education to back it up. However, upon recollection, nothing really came to mind in what to do. My mother wouldn't just accept "I'm quitting high school" without a backup plan. In a right mind, I wouldn't have given up all that was becoming for me. All that I ever wanted was recognition and respect on the basketball court. I made the paper for the last two months for scoring and now I was bored of it and I felt that I could do more.

My excuse to my coaches was that I was moving somewhere to have more of a challenge in basketball. My excuse to my mother was that I wanted to take courses in Scientology. I was hoping they could see it as following in their footsteps. My coaches accepted my statement in disbelief and probably didn't want my attitude around anymore, and my mother accepted my excuse too, probably to save me from anymore trouble in school. She wanted my high school diploma but could recognize maybe this wasn't the best time.

Before I replaced school with anything else I had some down time. I mostly roamed the city going to malls from one end to the other flirting with girls and getting numbers. A pile would amount on my dresser, not having interest to phone any of them, but stimulated at my new found ability to mingle with the opposite sex. I spent all the money in my account, mostly on music and challenged any guy who I passed with stare competitions. Late one night, I was walking to the convenient store with my brother and his friend. I saw two guys in the street. I already had an idea of who they were, as I lived in a small neighborhood. I was talking loud with my brother as I had been lately and when we passed them the one boy asked if I was talking to him. I wasn't, but I said that maybe I was. I knew both of them, although the one had a reputation for deplorable acts. There was a confrontation and I ended it verbally by yelling, "I know who you are and you ain't shit!" Spitting in his face. As I turned around I realized my mistake before I could turn back. He ended it physically, by whacking me with a blunt object that I would later realize was a lock wrapped in a bandanna. My knees buckled for a second and I rose again to see them walking off I could see his mouth moving with a final reply, but could not hear the words. My ears buzzed from the force to my head. This happened to be directly in front of my grade 11 math tutors' house. This could be symbolic of why you should stay in school; it was probably just a coincidence though. I stood there shocked from the trauma. The impact was so strong that I didn't feel the pain. I screamed for my brother and his friend to run home. I was afraid for them. I couldn't protect them anymore. As they left I stood and felt the blood run past my hat and down my head. I had passed out from much less before so I started sprinting home in fear of passing out and having no help. As I ran, I was in disbelief at what had happened since where I live is fairly peaceful. This guy had a bad track record however, and instantly blamed myself for turning my back on him. It turned out that I got home before them, the blood smearing the house before getting into the tub. I ran the water and called the ambulance. When my parents got home the medics were lowering me onto the stretcher. I was yelling at them to do it faster because I was on the verge of passing out and that feeling of nausea and motion sickness, plus the pain was not bearable.

This blow put me off my high horse for a little while, though a little undeserved. In the hospital I became a little more modest and blamed myself for knowing better. Everyone said it wasn't my fault and after examination I couldn't agree more. This made the anger thicken.

When I recovered a week or so later I went to see a friend at work. He worked at a gas station. That night I took it upon myself to steal some dirty magazines from the convenient store attached. The woman actually caught me and made me return them. She also banned me from the store. I got away with one and was looking at it talking to my friend. I noticed a crow bar he had in the gas station shop and I said I was going to borrow it. He didn't put up much of a fight and within minutes I was off to the guy's house who assaulted me, who I remembered just lived up the street.

I was told earlier that he was dragged out of bed that night by the cops. I wasn't sure if he was home or not I was just going. When I got to the house I crept around the opposite side of the street, still not sure what the hell I was doing. I peeked around the back and saw his sister with friends. I said that her brother was fucking dead, as I pounded the house with the crow bar. Still scared, I slammed the house a few more times as I ran away. When I was clear a friend of my family saw me walking with a crow bar in my hand thinking God knows what.

ChapTer eighT

→

I didn't begin a Scientology education right off the bat. My parents had been in talks with a teen counselor in Toronto who was also a Scientologist. She wasn't any kind of licensed counselor, but she worked at the YMCA and could get me playing with a lot of good basketball players. This was good enough for me at the time. I'd be staying with her as long as this worked out, which was also good for my parents who needed a break.

During a month or so we bonded talking about Scientology philosophies of which I knew enough about already to participate in deep conversations. We talked about basketball and life and ultimately got along. It was what I needed at the time, which was a friend, even if she was getting paid to be it. I told her about my ideas on life and my aspirations. She took most things I said lightly at first and humoured me, I believe. I was very sure (for a recent drop-out) of myself and explained all the things I had planned to do. It wasn't with confidence, but with ignorance that I would go on. I believed anything was possible, but of course what isn't, when a human being works hard. I would banter with no recognizance, only an empty assurance of self. I would expect things to happen because I was a bright vibrant young teen with everything to look forward to and the world was at my feet. I was talking about my dreams with no tentativeness, a feeling that everything would fall into place. The feeling of doubt and insecurity was void the very inkling that must be present to part confidence from arrogance. I would rant about all the things I wanted to do, when really they were all left behind in high school.

I didn't have much of a structured life staying in Toronto, as there was no strict schedule to follow. It was more filler time until my parents figured out what to do with me, or when I figured out what I was going to do with myself. I would go to the gym everyday with her, workout and play ball while she worked. I served as a kind of day against night on the courts, as I was the only white person in this area. It was the challenge I was looking for, however, and I became generally accepted and as time went on I blended in quickly. Black people seem to take better to arrogance then white people and a lot of it came as I got comfortable around them. I went from cracker to white boy, then Gottfried to yeah boy, in a fairly reasonable amount of time.

During this short period, I mostly roamed aimlessly getting lost in the big city of Toronto, which was foreign to me at the time. I would walk the malls several times over hinting at girls, occasionally snatching numbers. I was walking back to the subway one day when a man handed me a flyer and I looked at it. I then looked at the man then upward toward a building sign and said, "Oh, so I'm here, eh?" He asked me if I knew of the church and I told him that I was indirectly looking for it, which was a surprise for him to hear. I mean who looks for a church of any kind anymore? He said "Welcome" to which I replied. "I'll be back."

Over the next month or so I would go to the court and be fine, ready to socialize and play basketball. Sometimes I would be down, quite depressed, and the pent up stress and sadness would cause me to not be able to do anything effectively. I would go there sometimes on a weekend to try to get away from it all.

I wasn't sure what I had to escape from, so when I was there it didn't change anything. We would pick up friends to go play basketball and they would try talking to me in, and I could hardly muster a response. I was physically unable to speak due to tension. They'd ask my counselor what was wrong with me and she didn't really have a response either. If someone were to ask me what was wrong it was hard to answer because I genuinely didn't know. I knew I didn't want this feeling around me any longer. I was starting to accept myself as this person. This feeling wasn't as strong as before and would only last a day at a time now. In the back of my mind I thought maybe life didn't have to be like this and that maybe Scientology could make me the person I wanted to be.

A closed door to an achievable goal.
Could be the opening to a life. A change might be fearful.
But fear leads to death.
A stagnant existence might as well be.

ChapTer nine

The landlord at the counselor's place didn't find it convenient to have house guests anymore. I was becoming bored with the visits anyway. My Scientology teachings would now begin here at home. It was a small church and it was one on one, me and the instructor all afternoon. He worked for me everyday because I was the only person there. Once in awhile there would be someone else studying, but it was usually just me. He was there tirelessly for whatever they paid him per hour, which worked out to about 3 dollars at most. We got along and bonded: he made me think for myself and validated my thoughts.

I read quite a bit of literature and watched short films pertaining to Scientology in this little rotted out apartment that sat above a skuzzy downtown bar. I studied effortlessly while Will Smith's "Big Pimpin" would play from below, making it hard to concentrate. I believed in what I was learning, and this seemed like the important stuff: what we needed to know to survive   in this world. We would learn about people's emotional tones and where they stand on a scale of the highest form of living to death. There were even scales that went below death. I was taught about suppressive people, what made them suppressive, and how it affected us as human beings. I learned about how mental drive and motivation can affect a person physically. There were courses that involved drudging up the past in order to face it and acknowledge it, so that we can get over those times that may still affect us in the present. I learned that just because time has passed doesn't mean we've moved on. I found these, among many other practices, quite soothing and releasing. I saw a point to them - unlike school. Now that I see, I knew it was mostly lies, like all that math we "needed," all that science we would never use, and history that we were supposed to accept as true data. Furthermore, I learned that people believe religious scripture because they were told to. I was participating in an education and a religion based on logic and it felt true and I could see how it related to the problems of life.

In no time at all I had lost contact with any of my remaining friends from school. It didn't matter because I was on a different path, a better one. I was learning things that one could never learn in school. I was advancing and learning advanced things to which the caliber of only wise men knew. This information would be my savior and I would save many people with the knowledge I was gaining. However, when the window was cracked in that small classroom built for one, I could hear the Catholic kids laughing in the alley, and I couldn't help but feel sad and a little left out. When I would hear them at lunch I would look up from my studies, and even though I could not see them from the two story high complex, I gave a subtle look in the direction of my teacher, and he would glance back as if he knew what I was thinking. But this lost data that so many people were missing out on motivated me to keep going. I didn't want to go back to school, this was more important and this was my calling.

My instructor was an intelligent man and we talked about the world, mostly about the religion. We would talk as friends did, about music, how he'd been to 7 Tragically Hip concerts (a big Canadian rock band). I thought that a man as socially intelligent as well as intellectually able must be giving his life over to this cause for a reason. I soon started to think that there was no reason that I couldn't do the same thing. He would basically be my only friend for the next six months, this man who had at least fifteen years on me. I figured this left more room to grow and learn from his experience, since the information my father knew was always hush hush and too advanced for me, apparently.

As months passed I was learning a lot. I began to zip through the courses with ease. They aren't many people who can afford the courses one after another without having to work. It wasn't too long before my instructor and I were having deep philosophical discussions and I was challenging him and his views. This gave me more confidence. My IQ was going up, I was told because I was tested. This was a determining factor in my motivation. I felt dumb all through school, but here I understood more complicated theories and realized vast intricate plots to which most are people are spiritually ignorant. This could have been a personal coincidence, but he assured me that the school system and the teachers fail sometimes, and it wasn't my fault necessarily if I didn't understand something in school. He, like my father taught me how interest and usefulness have everything to do with learning. Henceforth, I would be taught new ways of comprehension in areas I was deeply inclined towards.

I read L. Ron Hubbard's words with such tenacity, while he sat there not overtly watching me, but not missing a thing. In

Scientology, while you are reading and you yawn it means you have a misunderstood word, unless of course maybe you haven't slept. He would always catch my yawn and say "Go back and look up your misunderstood." I would play it off always like I didn't, but sure enough there was always a word I couldn't fully define on my own, possibly coincidentally. After four months of consulting the dictionary I never felt such a surge of intelligence running throughout. People claim to speak and read a language or more than one. But what is more important? As Scientologists would say, would you rather be "glib" (ignorant) in five languages or fully competent in a predominant one? Words and meaning became everything, they even became scary sometimes because of how much emphasis was put on them, but I was pushed to move through them. I began to realize that the misunderstanding of language and words was important to all functions of mankind. The misunderstanding of all forms of communication seemed to be the ending of civilizations and the ending of individuals throughout time. Whenever we fail or quit something, it can usually be traced back to a misunderstanding of words or an inability to harvest them accurately. I could see that this was why teachers couldn't teach and illiterate people couldn't learn. When a word on a page is skipped or a concept, the whole section will become a lost cause. If we don't understand the word Sociology, for example, the whole course will be more difficult and less interesting and therefore impossible to master. In school, however, all we need to do is memorize certain things, which created a gap here and a gap there in a subject. Since we are memorizing and not learning, the data falls away after the test. This all seems dramatic and my obsession with the subject as time passed didn't help. But if you take 17 non-educational years spent with high school teachers thinking that you're dull, it's really quite easy to be fucking furious at how they thought you weren't teachable when in fact children love to learn. Any interested mind can learn vast amounts with a person capable and willing to teach.

Another way we learned was with plasticine. We would make demos of a scenario or idea to explain it in form, labelling each action to explain what it implied. It increased reality and a provided a clearer understanding sometimes. In Scientology, there was always a method of learning something to making sure it wasn't left misunderstood; it seemed like a cure for any starving mind. My earliest memory involving Scientology was from my childhood, when I was about four years old playing with plasticine. I was making a man and a dog at the old church which was only a block away from the one I speak of now. I came out of the demo room to a bunch of adults toasting around a mantel piece of a man's head. I was told it was L Ron's birthday and I assumed it was the man whose head I was looking at. I don't remember asking who he was. I suppose I kind of knew already. He was the founder of this place, the place my parents worked, maybe. I didn't know who Jesus was at this point so maybe that's the idea I got.

As I walked into my sanctuary now, though we didn't call it that, I looked into Hubbard's eyes every day, his head on a plaque watching over us as we carried on his legacy with his books spread all over the place and gathering dust. There weren't a large number of members here and they didn't have much money. The merchandise was left mostly unwatched because not many people ever came into the Church. As my 'wisdom' grew each day, I was angered that other people weren't benefiting as I was and that no one seemed to care.

Other exercises they liked to call training routines included being able to sit up in a chair across from someone eyes closed. You could call this a form of relaxing meditation. As you might notice, the general populous doesn't have very good confrontation skills. People lack confidence and don't generally look you in the eye much during communication or can't in fact communicate very well. I noticed this and it was a problem I had too. Another routine was sitting across from someone eyes open saying nothing for up to an hour at a time. Of course you don't want to stare at people but this raised an ability to confront, apparently, in terms of having an appropriate conversation with a human being, something people tend to shy away from these days. I recognized and understood the meaning for these things.

That intense, anxiety driven anger I had experienced subsided mostly for several months. I felt fairly calm and serene in the church; I was content with what I was doing since it served my needs. I still wouldn't get a job, except for a shady modeling job in town for some guy who charged a start up fee and wouldn't get us real paying jobs. It was an excuse for me to make out like I was doing something and to flirt with girls. Meanwhile in my off time, I would spend it at the mall flirting more and spending my life savings.

But day after day, all this talk and literature about ethics would get to me a little. I agreed with it, but it was hard to follow a strict set of rules when you're an eighteen year old guy. After awhile of being good and having no real friends there were nipping questions of whether I was doing the right thing and how much longer I could study Scientology, day in day out. Having to make money now or one day was over-shadowed by my father's wallet. There wasn't a lot of pressure on me because it was known that I wasn't entirely well and as long as I was doing "okay" (which meant not getting arrested), that was fine for now. I started to step out of my moral suit. Every week or so, as I walked home I would go into the downtown book store, keeping my bag up front. I would then go back to taking adult magazines and I would tuck them under my pants and shirt, grab my bag and walk out. I would feel bad after all I had learned that day in class. But I didn't have the moves quite yet to get any of these girls I knew alone, and also being to afraid to ask. So in that respect I didn't feel like this was causing the decay of Western civilization or even a crack in my religious endeavors.

When I did see my friends we would go to the strip club sometimes and one night a young dancer seemed to take an interest in me. I got her number and ended up getting a ride from my father to her place since he worked in her city. It's a fantasy for an 18 yr old to be invited to a strippers place and there a got a massage from her. When I proceeded, she told me she didn't want to cheat on her girlfriend. I found the experience queer in so many more ways than one, but overall for a young guy it was worth it. But I wouldn't say the fantasy panned out. I again spent the whole day at the mall after that waiting for my dad to get off work.

At home during this time my behavior was fairly manageable, at least I thought. The religion had calmed me down, although I was high at times at home and at the church, meaning that I was a bit overly excited and this was mostly due to the religion and all of the "realizations" I had about life on course. The spring in my step was starting to increase and I felt great. I was on the path of the wise and it didn't feel like anyone

51

could bring me down. If they could they'd be hard pressed to convince me to let them.

Cement blocks, Filled with chalk.
The young and the fun.
My lungs breathe in that sun.
I am reborn.
No one knows how good life could be.
My innocence is restored, I am becoming
free.

ChapTer Ten

❦

During this time I did manage to keep a couple friends for the odd time out to play basketball or use their connections to sneak a peak at a stripper, since I was underage. Whenever my personality seemed under wraps I would go out with my friends and get escalated again. They knew that I would be the one to get the ball rolling so they would encourage me, over and over. Some would even make up rumors and ideas to provoke me or feed me drinks, just to get me going, curios of what I would do.

One particular night I was sitting at home when I got a phone call. It was my best-friend of this group of companions. I supposed they had discussed it and he decided to phone me about the upcoming evening. He began to ask if I could take my parents van tonight so we could go around and throw eggs at things. I had taken the van once prior with them while we drank vodka and smoked weed. My friend had tried to drive us home, veering off the highway several times. I kept saying that I couldn't, trying to keep it down so my parents wouldn't hear. I kept hesitating and he kept persisting and that was all it ever took for me. Some coercing and pressure, along with encouragement was all a teenager usually needed and I was losing my rational self. Even though I was exhausted that night

53

because of lack of sleep catching up to me, I scooped up the keys, careful to be silent as I had before.

Assured that my parents wouldn't notice I took the car again. Although they didn't usually notice, I took one of the cars late after midnight with them being fast asleep. I was told that we would have it back quickly, and that we were just basically going for a ride and I was told to come in ten minutes. So I did, backing out of the drive-way with my parents potentially able to see, my judgment coming and going, coming and going further down.

I pulled up to my friend's house. They poured out of the house excited at my expense. They came into the van with smiles which matched mine, but theirs were distant because they were hiding their anxiety about this night. I had soon decided to not let it bother me and I would rest. I let my friend drive the van. They went to pick up eggs and whatever other supplies they needed and they cruised throughout the city, assaulting the houses of enemies and innocent cars, anything they wanted. I would lay in the back mostly unimpressed with the headphones on, blaring music, dosing off from pure exhaustion.

I didn't know how far we had gone or where we were. I wasn't interested and I couldn't stay awake. When the car would stop or accelerate I would wake to my music and look up. When the car stopped the last time I opened my eyes and could see what looked like a siren flashing on the interior roof. I sat up and turned around, my music still blaring to see a university security car sitting still behind us. I took off my headphones to hear my friends talking back and forth hurried and worried. I remember being calm and thinking to myself, what could these toy cops do for a practical joke as innocent as throwing eggs.

The next thing I knew the cops were inside the car asking questions. I was being sarcastic and non-cooperative. My friend was surprised at what little threat the security was posing to me. My best friend kept on telling me to calm down and to be quiet. But I felt it was necessary to make it known to these cops what little they could do to me and who I was. I had no mental function because of the exhaustion to see any threat from any security guards.

Before I knew it I was in a locked holding area, like an interrogation cell. I had no idea how I got there as my memory faded from mental exhaustion. I wasn't really sure how my friends let me get in a security cell at 1 a.m. in the morning but I wasn't upset. I remember waking up from a nap in there, still having my disc-man on I started singing away to the music without a care. We didn't intake anything that night, but I was definitely high from being over-tired. I was just so sure this wasn't a big deal. I was sure the consequence would be minimal.

I eventually was taken out to see both my parents there and my friends sitting in chairs in a hallway. My parents, as they walked in saw my friends sitting there, my mother giving my buddies dirty looks, knowing I had been talked into it at least partially by them. I had no idea why they were outside and I was being held captive. Before my release my parents had already had a chat with the head of security. The charge of grand theft auto was being discussed. My mother was explaining that she didn't want to press any charges. He rebutted that he could, and in fact might, press charges himself. She went on to say that it wasn't necessary because they had been looking into a place to send me and keep me out of trouble and get me some help. He would go on to inform her that it would be a good idea and, if in fact she did this, there would be no action taken.

I was described as unattached or disconnected from myself or the night's consequences as I was taken home. I wasn't quite in there, as I hadn't slept for a long period of time, which made me lost in my own conscience, coming and going lapses of extreme energy to above average energy. This behavior was more common in me lately; being more aware at times and then gone on a dream like getaway to others. A parental punishment wasn't going to happen because they already realized that no good would come from it. They established that I was unwell and they needed a break as a last resort, which would only be the beginning.

About a week passed while my parents discussed my fate and I spent more time doing nothing. Nothing besides obsessively thinking, lying and embellishing everything I talked about, having bouts of grandiose feelings, and visiting all the people I knew all the time. I remember everyday feeling as though I had accomplished a lot. Whatever I did I felt I did it well. My thought process was spot on, I was teaching myself new and useful knowledge, and I was having my own cognitions that no one else knew about. I was convinced I was special because other people didn't think these things. I thought I was on a special mission possibly from God or Angels to educate people against their ignorance. The only production was a mass of thoughts and new ideas with no solutions that I knew of. If I couldn't place the thoughts, then more thoughts had to be invented to explain these. I needed constant messages and answers - I couldn't rest until my mind had produced an answer sufficient enough to let the rest of me back off. If my mind could not expose the answers to life's impossible questions I would press on, if nothing else came, my psyche would naturally forget to save my mind power, only to think something else. Rest was not an option.

I was called in the kitchen to speak to my parents. They started to speak candidly about how things weren't going too well lately. That maybe I needed a break from things. They went on to tell me about a place in New Mexico for Scientologists, a ranch that was kind of like a "luxury resort" and a place to relax. There were nature trips that I could experience while riding horses, with beautiful scenery and basketball. I'd have a chance to be with young people like me who were interested in Scientology and I could learn more about it there. I wasn't sure at first about being torn away from everything that was here. Like the flip of a coin that my mind had been like recently, I saw that maybe I didn't have much going for me here, and that I could help people at this ranch learn more about spirituality, while also getting to take a trip. It wasn't a day before I was packing my things.

ChapTer eleven

Once we reached New Mexico there were two men waiting for me. We met cordially and off we went to the fairly remote valley where I was going to stay. The drive was a good distance and we made small talk, but mostly I kept quiet. Near the destination I asked to stop for a gatorade and beef jerky. I should have taken a hint that maybe this wasn't the luxury resort getaway I thought it was going to be, since he subtly sighed at my request and the overall disinterest of the car trip.

When we got there I was explained the rules by the head of staff. A stiff bitch it was apparent right away. Basically, she explained that we could phone home once a week basically and the calls were supervised. I didn't see the need for this, but listened on. She told me that if the conversation on my part began to be inaccurately or defaming to they're organization, the call would be disconnected. I didn't see how she could do this since my parents were paying good money. But, I was here now and there was no going back anytime soon.

Before I even got situated there was this punk rock kid but mostly a punk, who came up behind and tried to grab me. I knocked him six feet backwards putting the back my arm against his neck. I asked him what was going on? Then he put me in a headlock to initiate his dominance over me. I didn't fight back. I just sat in the lock, not sure what to do or what kind of behavior this was. Another kid in the room then said "Just tap or say I give" So I gave and he let go. I asked him what that was about and he didn't really have a response, just an ignorant sly smile. After a snack I went to bed that night with about 7 other boys in the room. Uncomfortable is probably an understatement. I thought someone might try to hurt me as I slept, but that didn't occur. Day by day the boys would get in arguments usually with me and it was settled by the wrestling tap out matches outside. No one seemed to like me because I would assume I appeared to be a cocky kid from Canada and to them didn't belong there. This would eventually become clear when they realized I actually liked Scientology.

Most of the kids were there because they had to be, not unlike my case. But most of them were heavily into drugs or crime and had some sort of record. I was here to avoid getting one. These kids weren't interested in learning Scientology ways they were just kids of Scientologists. I think they despised me for being book smart and interested in Scientology, and I despised them for being criminals or whatever they were there for. Maybe I did think I was better than them at the time, but I thought I was better than most people now.

As a few days passed it was plain to see it wasn't going to be the accommodating trip as was explained. We had work to do during the day and classroom in the evenings. The lessons consisted of Scientology courses. Not long after I was there, I spent one particular day and most the night gathering and stacking wood for camp. This was something us newbies had to do. It rubbed me the wrong way that we had to do this while the rest of the kids celebrated Halloween indoors without us and also that I had to be here with strangers during it, working of all things. At a boot camp I would presume being called maggot and doing push ups but this was just as irrational.

Nothing was very structured there. There wasn't much supervision over us. The kids would take out their frustrations on me and I would feed it, being very good at targeting the core of their anger. Sometimes in the heat of an argument we would go out to wrestle, this way dominance and violence could be established without punishment. I would mostly overpower the kids with a size advantage, but take it easy and end the fight early not being a violent person by nature. In the end the kids would gang up on me and take shots holding me down, then scurry off. I was not able to tell who did it really.

On some nights I would seek refuge in the adult quarters where they would sometimes watch Scientology videos. I would feel safe there away from any trouble. As the adults gasped at the footage of cruel tortures psychiatrists would engage on their patients I would do the same. Seeing all the mind control techniques, the altering of brains, lobotomy's and psychotropic drugs. I, along with my fellow Scientologists was appalled. They however, didn't know yet I was one of them. These educational videos were meant for us to make a difference and to help the world or even save it. No Scientologist ever questioned that these videos we watched were more than 40 years old and quite obsolete. I don't know why. The videos were to make it relate to today like nothing has changed.

The classroom is where I wanted to shine and show what I had learned and how capable I was of learning more. All around I was disinterested in the physical work they had for me to do. Mostly busy work, I thought. The physical work was 50 percent of the way to get out of there. I figured if I showed my Scientology devoutness I would find a way out. It wasn't just that, but I had no motivation to do work for them. My parents were paying them a large amount of money for what? For me to scrub their shower, where most of the boys had just freshly jerked off that morning anyway. No, I didn't think so. I was going to get something out of this. I would cruise through as many Scientology courses as I could to add to my resume and to advance up the Scientology ladder. If that wasn't enough I would find a way out of there.

The frustration grew everyday. Little comments, arguments and young animosity's. We would play basketball and whenever I was about to score I'd be pushed or fouled hard on purpose. I would jump up for a lay up and be pushed in the air. "Do you want to fucking die?" I would scream. One of them would say sorry won't happen again and it would. They had the advantage of numbers also. It didn't help either that I was pulled aside and told that being the oldest and technically an adult at eighteen I could be criminally charged if I hurt these boys, who were mostly only a year younger. There was a lot going on inside my head, but I knew that wouldn't be good and the thought of being away from home for even longer scared me. It also scared me to not be able to defend myself. The only thing that could have felt like home there, was a civilized basketball game of normal street ball and that never could play out right. It was these accumulating reasons that I would boast to these boys that I wasn't staying here long. They laughed hard at me, saying that no one leaves, and no one escapes until they have finished the program. We would make bets with the few possessions we had, whether or not I would make it out of there. Of course boys will talk, but if I made it out of here I wouldn't have time to collect my winnings. I would just be gone, probably leaving behind my own things.

Little by little my suitcase became lighter and things went missing. I didn't notice because mentally I was still here and there out of it, sometimes euphoric, going to bed last and getting up first. I hadn't had rest in a long time. Mornings, I would watch the sun rise over the mountains, a scenery at least I had not been used to. My only sense of sanity (even though I wasn't quite right in the head) being my disc man still, as I would make my way down to the horses stables and sing to them every morning. Feeling as though and hesitating to know that they were my only friends in the world.

During a night early on, I wandered outside the facilities where two of the boys were waiting. The same boy who had initiated me called me over. I had no problem as I wanted to make the best of the situation I was in. When I got over, I saw he had what looked like a metal rod in his hand. He began to threaten me with it, continuously faking to strike me every time I didn't answer as he felt fit. He coerced me away from the other boy around to a corner and told me to kneel down. As I hesitated he became more insistent with the metal rod. After I did, he looked down and I did also to see that he already had his penis out. I began to rise to my feet and asked what he was doing in a nervous tremble. To which he raised his weapon again then started laughing. Laughing in a sick self-satisfying way I didn't think any 16-year-old was capable of owning.

For the first time my nerves were a little shot. I wasn't sure what to do or if this was going to get worse. Was anyone going to help or protect me? Or was I going to have to get violent or leave somehow. I pondered what to do in the garage having a cigarette that a boy had given me. I wasn't sure how to think this out. I didn't even know where I was. I was holding a crow bar in my hand from the garage and shaking. A service man came up behind me and said "Hello." I jumped up startled and almost hit him with it. He asked if I was alright to which I lied and told him I was. I reported the incident to a kind woman I had met and trusted. She did what she could. The boy would only be taken to "camp" as they called it, which he was used to by now, for unruly behaviour. It was a trailer 40 feet from our cabin. That night however, the boy lay fast asleep already separated from the rest of us, but still in our barrack's. This was until they prepared camp for him.

The anger and nervous tremors were brewing inside of me. Earlier that night I had picked up a rock from outside and stuck it inside my jacket. After lights out I sneaked past the overnight watch office and waited for the security officer to take his rounds outside. As he did, I stood over this boy and held the rock to his head. I watched him peacefully sleep as if he didn't have a care in the world. I truly believe he didn't, as psychopaths never do they're always undeniably justified in their own actions and they just don't have a conscience. I looked over this boy with his life in my hands knowing that a personality this young and twisted wouldn't change. Not when it was so out of whack already. In two minutes I thought about all the other people he would invade and reap havoc upon throughout the rest of his life. I wanted to end that before it began. I was religious now, but not ignorant, I felt some people shouldn't be here and I wanted to snub him out. The miserable soul he was, I could sense it from the first day. God, give me the strength to make this his last.

I raised the rock up to strike it down across his head. My chest began to deep breathe silently knowing I couldn't wake anyone including him. He was the type of boy that would be a man someday; lying, cheating, stealing, raping, maybe even murdering. I had never hated someone's soul as I did his. I wanted to smash his teeth out and lay a final crushing blow to his skull. I began to think that maybe I wasn't leaving here and I was being treated like a criminal anyway. So take him out and do this earth a favour. I then lowered the rock and walked away smiling at the thought of what could have been.

Of course violence breeds violence. It was becoming more apparent that I didn't belong here and that this was the wrong choice. I believed I was an intellectual spirit on the path of righteousness and enlightenment. I began to breeze through the Scientology courses again doing one or two a week when most the kids were still working on their first. I was reading the books in my spare time also. I still continued to dismiss the labour work because I didn't care about it. They would make me once and awhile but I hardly did it to they're approval.

No one seemed to care about my opinions in the classroom. If the kids were even listening they didn't understand, being half illiterate. On an ordinary evening the course room supervisor stood up front to start the class and asked, "Does anyone know what tone 0.0 is?" Without a hand up I told him that it was body death. Trying to imply also that I was close to it being here or that I wish I could kill someone. He replied, "Um, no." and flipped to the page he had marked for the lesson and did a turn around saying that it was body death. I wasn't sure how he presumed to ask and get an answer for this, from a bunch of teens who could barely think for themselves yet and didn't care about Scientology, especially when he didn't know it himself. So it did make sense when he looked at me funny for knowing this. This made me feel that a Scientology instructor was no more knowledgeable than a teacher and my interest started to dwindle when the instructor's animosity towards me raised.

A person's tone in Scientology involves being in a fixed mood in the present time. This is something they figure out with questions and observing a persons behavior in order to bring them up to the next highest tone through processes. Wherever someone is on a tone chart they will either ascend or decline to the next level on the chart. For example; emotionally, if a person was in a state of pain, when they got up to a state of boredom there would most likely be an antagonism or sarcastic period first. When someone is sympathetic they will experience grief before they would ever spiral down towards apathy. However most people sit in what is called a fixed tone. The tone which is natural with their personality.

Back to the tone of 0.0, which was body death. The tone scale went beyond and even below that into what can happen after death, or if you will the after-life. This wasn't indicating heaven, but a confused state of the soul after death; understandably . Scientology never gave any opinion against heaven or hell. It was said the after-life will be made upon the decision of the person or soul depending on what they think they deserve. The after-life was beginning to sound fairly good to me at this present moment in time.

The truth was, I didn't know where I belonged. It wasn't here and it wasn't anywhere. I didn't belong home either. I was doing well here in studies and doing bad everywhere else. The kids made me feel like an outsider because I hadn't been that bad. If I was singling myself off I didn't notice. Even the course supervisor and the staff supervisor were condescending . I don't think they enjoyed my questions, there were too many, and beyond their scope. I was the only kid there willing to learn and instead of nurturing that I believed it scared them. They didn't know what to expect when I came, and my interest in education they had no care for because it lead to questioning them. Of course I wasn't easy to get along with always and was difficult. I was confused and had a tireless amount of energy. It was as if there was something they didn't want me to find out.

The course supervisor was apparently at a level in the religion that was called OT 8 ; this was an abbreviation for "operating thetan." The "operating" meaning functional and the "being" an ancient Greek word for the soul. So in other words, attaining this level meant you were a capable spirit or person. My father was also OT 8 and at this time the levels went up to eight. Apparently there were higher levels coming out, which lead me to wonder if they were holding them and if so why. And if they were being invented that would be impossible since the founder is no longer with us. An OT was someone I was supposed to look up to and learn from, but this man, my teacher in New Mexico, seemed to have no wisdom to offer and didn't seem interested. This didn't bother me because I knew the quote from Hubbard in Dianetics. "A cleared cannibal is still a cannibal." (Clear also being a state achieved before OT meaning the mind no longer controls you.) The quote meaning you can help a person to be the best they can be, but of course nothing more. All the education in the world won't necessarily change a human-being who is dull by nature. (Just like priesthood doesn't make you holy if you're being unholy with children). My motivation to spiritual enlightenment wasn't altered because I was me. I was not yet deemed an OT, but I already felt I was thinking on the level. I was on the path to being a Scientologist to the utmost standards. I just had to get the fuck out of here.

Outside the indoors, But still four walls.
Inside and outside, Hope falls.
What little is left inside, Will be the dictator of your life.
Two fates:
The one you precipitate, And the one you escape.

ChapTer Twelve

I began to get sent to camp, that trailer outside for my behaviour. I refused to do labour work most the time and was put there where we did nothing, except when we weren't scraping that rust of the metal stables with rocks. It was a useless task just made for busy work. I was put there alone or with anyone else who had done something wrong. Often it was too cold to sleep and no one gave me extra blankets. There was no running water and I could not leave. When everyone was asleep, I would often go inside where there was a fire and talk all night with the security man, since sleep was the last thing on my mind. I was running short of a lot of the basic necessities, but I was in my own world a bit too much to notice. People would complain about my body odor sometimes, but no one would go into town and get me deodorant. A counselor would tell me to scrub or he'd come in and scrub for me, on my way to the shower. Something he might have enjoyed I guess. Of course all the showering wouldn't help with no deodorant. I would have to use other people's sometimes when they were not around and steal people's batteries for my Walkman to get by. During camp there was a port -o- potty I would have to use and groups of boys would come in and tip it over with me in it. My patience sliding, I took up smoking out of boredom and it was giving me a little head buzz. A short- lived initial inhale taking me away for only a moment, I would start to long for.

Coming onto the landscape some evenings I would see a counselor and some of the boys riding horses through the trail. I didn't know why I couldn't be on the horses. I was so lost, I don't even remember asking. I was soothed by the presence of the horses. As I walked them back, this experience reminded me of a past life supposed memory, déjà vu, of me leading a group of men on a mission or back home from one. A life, memory of when I was important and in a power position, maybe. How does one in an altered state differentiate between reality and imaginary? It would become increasingly difficult in time.

Too tired to express anger and too angry to give a shit, my patience began to wane. I hadn't slept for seven months or longer really and I would gear in and out of climactic moods, being submissive and then overly aggressive. One day shortly after I saw that a boy had a DMX C.D. I took it and played it in the barracks without him knowing, He came back in and asked who played it. I gave him a sneaky smile and when he came over he proceeded to choke me, up against the wall. I just stared at him as if to say I don't care and you can't hurt me. I would've like to hit him but I'd been playing psychological head games with these undereducated kids for a month now. I was also afraid of backlash. I was against the wall smiling aware that if I lost it, I might go too far and welcomed the pain. Yet the next day another kid said something derogative to me because I had just acted like a rug all this time. I round-housed kicked him in the gut and he stopped breathing. I got on top of him and started coming down on his ribs with my knees. I felt bad after because I wasn't like these kids, but someone had to get it.

I couldn't fight everyone though and the threat of unknown American criminal charges still haunted me. I was alone. The kind lady counselor had left back to California. My one buddy there had left to go back home for awhile. I didn't understand why everyone had forsaken me. Was I that different? Was it because I was Canadian? Or a Scientologist? I couldn't understand why a Scientology organization would make a fellow member feel segregated even if I was troubled. I couldn't see it as much as an outside onlooker, but I was still in my right mind. Some what.

I wouldn't cry as I wasn't sane enough to cry anymore and I wouldn't do it here and show weakness. Fuck these criminals. Even the counselors were criminals at one time most likely, and that's why they were here. Who are they to look down on me? Criminals don't coexist with the honest; this fact was becoming clear to me. They could rot in their self-made hells for all I cared. This sense of undeserved rejection and cruelty was pushed away into my subconscious. I didn't want to face this as I had my last year in school. Was it me? If I were to leave here would any place be any different? I battled some days knowing I was on a different and much higher plateau of intellect than others and then questioning whether there was something wrong with me. The days between highs and lows would be a cloud of confusion and doubt, triggering insecurity that could only lead a build up of fake ego in order to survive.

The absence of stability bred an absence of fear. Nothing was really right or heading that way. I felt I had a future, but it wasn't to be switched on by this place. I was living in a cabin in bunk beds with other boys and my parents were paying thousands for non-existent help they couldn't observe. They wouldn't approve if they could see this, and I knew this. With no real way to contact them and no way to convince them, it was in my own hands: I could be here a year or more. Having nothing to lose and more importantly nothing to gain anymore, my attitude changed and I started to follow rules a little more. I started to act a little as if I was going along with the program as was designed for me. I didn't want anyone to suspect anything. I wasn't ever a bad person and therefore didn't need correction. I felt fine and would obviously feel great outside this place. The rule that no one leaves here without significant change would not apply here because I felt there was nothing wrong with me. I didn't have a criminal mind. Just had an accident and lost my way a couple times. I wanted to contribute to the world and they wanted to treat me like a write-off.

ChapTer ThirTeen

Time was all I had here, but it was running out for me. When a C.D. of mine went missing I would enjoy the one I had to the fullest. The music took me away and I experienced it as if every second was my last breath. As I held on to my Scientology books I gripped every word even harder. The text compelled me to have hope for every new day, even though they were all the same here. I would pretend to exteriorize (a term in Scientology for the soul leaving the body through death, sleep or through a higher awareness and consciousness) and escape my own trappings externally and internally. My thoughts were rapid and cycling, sure and then not. Anger and hatred clashed with hope. The only reason I still smiled was because daily I learned that I was bigger than this situation and that justice always prevails in the end. These presumptions were in my readings. Negativity is never constant unless you provoke it. Life ebbs and flows. The problem of consistent thought would always break in overstating my hope. I was not in control of my life anymore and this hope I acquired relates to a life a person owns. Knowing whether the move forward and finish this program or skip out early was the question.

Frustration amounted and anxiety started to kick in heavily. I would go into fits of rage and angry tirades after a group would gang up on me physically or verbally. If I actually did try to masturbate as all us teenage boys did, I would be interrupted. The poorly built wooden door on the bathroom would give way to sneak peeks and a dumb fuck counselor posing as my mentor, calling me out on it and embarrassing me, presumably trying to watch. I was just trying to squeeze out one short moment of ecstasy from this hell hole with my so very gratifying Sears catalogue. So instead, I stole a pack of one boy's cigarettes and hid myself away for a half hour chain smoking. At this point that being the only claim of revenge to the world I could muster.

A cigarette smoking away like the mechanics of my speeding mind, I sat in silence. Enjoying this moment as much as possible, I always cherished my alone time, but here it was all too sublime. I would have just as much time as it took for them to notice I was gone. On the ranch I would tuck myself far off in the cow pasture watching the cows look at me nervously. Realizing that they weren't as nervous as I was, and seeing that my life was as pointless as their own, or even more right now, triggered a shift in my mental gears.

It was announced. We were going on a camping trip, all of us together. How sweet, I thought. Every bad childhood memory pertained to a camping trip (no sodomy implied). I was never an outdoorsy type of kid and being with these kids and wild animals within the rugged nature it would be hard to tell the difference. Nevertheless, we were off before I could pack, and since there wasn't much left to pack it was just as well.

A bus took us on the main road out a little and into the Rocky Mountains a small distance away. We found a flat area where I suppose they set camp every time they decided the boys needed a soulful nature journey. I was dreading this even more until we made camp. The clean air and the fresh swaying trees shot me an ounce of relief. As the first night bonfire blazed I found a little of myself again, the patience and hope for another day and the fierce competitor as the flames reflected a burning in my eyes.

That night I slept.I was up first the next morning as usual, warming up to the remains of last night's fire. I was eventually greeted with some compassion by the course supervisor as he offered me some of his trailer brewed coffee. He gave me what was left of it which was only a few sips; it wasn't much of an offer, was even kind of an asshole gesture. But I saw it as a sign of maybe a turning point: I had officially spent a decent and tolerable 24 hours with everybody. I sipped my coffee with an internal peace coming over me and a misty morning gray fog that soothed and regenerated my thoughts, the cool and invigorating air purifying my body and giving way to a delusional sense of freedom and almost independence.

It was getting colder and the mountains seemed dreams away from the desert type area we had cohabited in. There was snow now all over the place. A few days had passed and aside from a few wrestling matches and some verbal battles, nothing had gone wrong. In fact everything was normal per what was given. I had been primarily quiet and had kept to myself just trying to get through this I had this. I would stay hush, hush until someone said something really stupid, but of course that was most likely much more often than I can remember.

My animosity came back to its fullest when I realized that the punk kid who needed a beating rather than help was gone. I was told that he was back at the ranch receiving auditing. Auditing is, you could say, the most important process in Scientology. It is an act by which a trained person sits one on one with the audited person and asks him or her questions

74

which relate to difficulties and barriers in that person's life. The goal is to get the person to confront unwanted memories (even in their past life) to increase the person's ability to move on from them. This positive outcome is demonstrated by the person's up-lifted mood afterwards. This process is done with a contraption called the E-meter. The audited holds cans, which send their energy or negative energy, called "mass," through the E-meter machine and the dial will show a positive or negative charge, which actually pertains to the mind. When the person's subject reads less charge there is less energy fixated on this negative problem. While it is obvious that not facing your fears might weigh you down in life, this "charge" apparently when deleted lessens the body mass of an individual. This is all mental energy and energy itself we are talking about. Matter is condensed energy which has charge and mass. In all actuality the E-meter is an archaic form of the same type of technology like a lie detector machine. There is an endless array of questions and processes mocked up so that when you are tackling an "issue" it would give you the feeling that you conquered it when the needle clears leaving people euphoric often. This is the brainwashing addiction. The processes never stop and you are always close to your "huge potential as a spirit."

It crazed me to find out that this kid was receiving help when I wasn't. I hadn't been audited yet and I deeply wanted to be. Auditing was going to make me better than ever. It was going to make me be able to get out of here and live a successful life. Along with my love for the education it was a winning combination. The kid didn't even want help, but they told me it was the only thing that was going to help him. But I didn't buy it. I wanted the help and I didn't even think there was that much wrong with me, but I wanted to improve. That kid didn't care whether he lived or died, sinned or lied. Scientology taught us that everyone can be helped and saved who wanted to be. They never talked about making efforts for deviants. For all I cared, they could cast him down with the American government's experimental psychiatrists and lobotomize his ass.

ChapTer fourTeen

The sun broke free from the mountains again, unfortunately dawning another day. As the day moved on, it warmed up and the sun light beamed off the ground and rocks; covered in snow. I noticed that the punk kid had been brought back to camp at some point and had a black eye. I asked him what happened and he told me to mind my own business and I smirked. One of the kids had apparently done what I had wanted to do, but was too scared to or wasn't allowed to do, whichever will suffice. My mood had started to climb for not only that reason, but it was almost time for lunch served out of the trailer. We gathered around for grub and in no time it was devoured with everyone just hanging around with not much to do.

Once our food was served, the counselors went back in their trailer to do whatever they did and we were left to do nothing. In the afternoon delight, one of the kids threw a snowball at me somewhat playfully and so I threw one back. One by one the kids all started throwing them at me and soon there were ten kids hurling snow and ice at me. One of the snowballs came into fierce contact with my crotch. I gripped my package and face and started to walk away from the situation, the snowball ratio decreasing with every step, but my rage was increasing. I made my way to the camp site area where our tents were and I looked back only to see one of the kids within my eye sight. I kept walking and I could see that he was watching me. I didn't understand why I couldn't be left alone. How much patience did I have to have? I looked back again and he was still watching me, wondering why I was going so far beyond the tents. I looked back one more time knowing he would mention my little walk (which was even too much freedom for me to have) in 3 seconds, so I booted it with my heavy mountain boots leading my trail. I heard five steps into it, the kids yelling, "He's running!!" and I literally started running for the hills and for my life.

After hearing the yelling I looked back again to see three people running after me. At this point I cut a hard left up one of the mountains. Determined to never see them again and for them not to have the satisfaction of finding me, I hightailed it up the hillside with all the ferocity I could muster, barreling over rocks and trees big and small. I could hear them on my tail, like a pack of wolves hunting out of boredom and humiliation instead of sustenance. I high-geared it more and added in many zigzags and cross directions staying off the paths and before long not only had I lost them, but I was lost myself.

When I took off I had thought there was civilization on the other side of the mountain and that would be my escape. I thought this from judging the bus ride in, because it didn't seem that far and by my calculations it was in this direction. If I had been right, the confusion of the chase had led me astray. If I had even remembered that these were the Rockies, it was too late now to go back and even this was worth some alone time at least right now. Not sure of which way to walk I did just that, when I couldn't run anymore. Shortly after, I started on the path again which was any ground between the mountains since it was a smoother terrain. If they found me I would hide or run again.

Early on into the search the two youngest boys in the program had spotted me from the top of the hills. They hadn't said anything to anyone right away for some reason. They would later be made to write their "overts" (A Scientology term for a wrong doing , and by writing it down is bringing the act to the physical world, this is considered a proper admittance and therefore relieving guilt) down back at the ranch. Not long after this I had heard ATV four wheelers out searching for me. I didn't know what would become of this, but putting some of the pressure on them instead of me was a bit of a rush. My life had been put in their hands and I was out of sight. The freedom of being loose and observing the beautiful scenery with these mountains seemed like a vacation for the first time, but with intense stress in the back of my mind.

Like any instant gratification of a high this soon came down. Realizing that I was utterly alone and this time in the middle of nowhere, four hours into the walk I sat down and cried. Searching, maybe, praying for help from my deceased grandpa who I believed might be looking over me. I got up quickly and wiped my eyes, knowing I had to keep on, to find a way out since I didn't hear the ATVs anymore. I must have wandered even further away at this point not having any clue where to go. Not long after my prayer I was cursing God and daring him to bring his best because I didn't give a fuck anymore. "Fuck you God, is this all you got? You fucking prick, are you happy now? Is this the best you can do you pussy?" I would scream and snivel, looking up at the sky saying, "fuck you" over and over again. Then silently a few minutes later, I was taking it back just in case he did exist and was planning to call my bluff.

Scientology never spoke much of God, but implied a supreme being. Either way, when we are desperate, praying is an idea ingrained into us when we are young – the idea that God is testing or punishing us.

After calming down I would regain composure and start walking faster. When I got thirsty I would climb partially up a mountain and delve into the rocks where within them would be holes. The holes had frozen over and I had to punch through the ice and suck the water out that lay underneath. I had on a warm enough jacket so I was sweating, but it was too cold to take it off. As the sun was quickly drawing to dusk, it was becoming colder by the minute. My sweat started to freeze to my body.

Fearing the night, I rushed faster to find smaller mountains that seemed to have an opening above that could be an opening into civilization, which seemed to be another world at this point. I climbed quickly up them just to climb back down seeing nothing, but more of the same scenery. I came across a form of tree that was foreign, and the only source of what could possibly be food here. Some type of a berry that almost had the texture of a nut. I could've just as easily been eating something poisonous, but I needed something to move on, not eating too much in case they were harmful. My hopes were starting to get grim and by this time I was screaming for help, but the sounds of my search team or I should say hunters were miles away now. The only sound I was about to hear now were the wolves haunting howl on this rocky night.

As the impending night drew chillingly closer I thought of building a little cove out of sticks. I would rather have had a lighter to set them on fire along with the two cigarettes I had in my pocket that would go unsmoked. I saw no point in the boy scout method because pulling that off was doubtful. So I kept walking, inching through the darkness until I could barely see in front of me anymore. I wandered around, disorientated from shock and the dropping temperature, finally reaching a small opening in a mountain where the moon shone through, reflecting off of some water that sat in a rock alcove on the ground. I couldn't walk in a straight line anymore and this area was at least a little brighter. So, I set up camp by kneeling down and lying beside a rock. As I tried to sleep the moon's face kept changing from stern looks to taunting smiles. I could not stand this anymore so I closed my eyes and fell asleep eventually, shivering violently.

A cry, a scream or a prayer, Will always make someone aware.

When you are alone, More alone than you can bare.

No one ever wants to care. This is why you are there.

ChapTer fifTeen

→

I awakened into anxiety I too quickly remembered and a conscious reality that I couldn't forget too soon. My eyes dreaded seeing what I knew was there before they opened. I was not overly thankful that a bear or a mountain lion didn't tear me to shreds in my sleep because I was still here. The sun had barely risen, but there was enough light to continue my quest since it was too cold to do anything, but to walk to increase circulation warmth. I tripped to my feet and stumbled with every step ahead, noticing how much damage the cold had done to my body. I had to get moving and the only thing I had to look forward to was the sun rising so my body could regenerate its heat.

There was no idea what direction to go so I carried on towards the sun because it seemed warmer that way. The plan was to walk even faster than I had yesterday to find a way out of here. As my bones warmed up my pace became faster. Through motivation to escape, I ran a lot of the time. I took little breaks to sob or rest, but not for long. As the day drew on, I passed areas that I swore I had already traveled through. This panicky frustration forced me to run frantically for a way out, but my feet were cut badly because I had no socks on and the chaffing was starting to burn. Finding my way to a flat open area I climbed up as big of a mountain as possible to see over. I found only dead ends. On the mountain I heard and then saw a plane overhead and ran to an open area. Flailing and raising my arms I ran to the middle of the area and jumped-up and down. I came down into the very centre of the low plain to appear more visible and once the plane had passed, I lay down on my back.

It wasn't a rescue plane and I lay there for another 15 minutes partly out of defeat and partly in hope that he dispatched someone to get me. When another passed over me in the sky I did nothing, since I was only an ant among mountains and the sky. Coming to that conclusion, I knew I got myself here and I'd have to get myself out. I could die soon, but I didn't want the searchers to find me and bail me out anymore. I would be the first person to escape this camp. That's what I said in the beginning and if this is the end result to beat them, so be it. People die in the name of being right everyday and we must be careful what we wish for. Trained, experienced, outdoors men die out here in the mountains every year. I had only my stubbornness, irrationality and ignorance to depend on here.

Getting to my feet I chose a direction and proceeded into the mountain forest terrain. Some moments were heightened by feelings of self-delusional independence, as though this was the first time I was really on my own. As the day went on, I came across the tracks of the four-wheelers that had been searching for me and the scenery started to look familiar. Had they stopped looking for me? The thought didn't soothe me now and I wouldn't put it past the pricks. If I died out here they would have a serious problem. So too would I if I had to spend another night out here and the thought of the cold sent chills up my spine as I walked on blindly with tears drowning my vision.

The rest of the day consisted of more emotional ups and downs, and the night was inching closer. I knew that if the night came I would collapse in grief. There would be no point to go on and I would have no choice but to lay like a log until another pointless day began or until the cold chilled my nervous system to shut down. I was desperate now to find a path leading to somewhere and I ran until my feet gave in to the pain. Walking around a mountain I came around a corner in a sprint when I suddenly saw a stretch of the trail leading into what looked like a road. I checked my eyes and did a double take. I started to skip along up to it and dance a little in triumph of my discovery. As I pranced up the road I knelt down and buried my face in a big muddy puddle and drank the dirty water. It tasted like victory.

For four more hours I walked up this path to a supposed way out. I kept telling myself I was bound to come across something soon. Nothing kept coming. Until suddenly over a hill came a truck. Moving to the side I watched it intently. I almost put my arm up to flag it down then thought against it since I would have to come across a town soon. Then the truck stopped because no one was ever out here and I noticed a shotgun sitting on the dashboard. It was an older couple and the man rolled down his window and asked me where I was going. I played it off as no big deal, that I was just following the path out of here. They informed me that I was just going further up into the mountains and there was nothing there. With this news and the night falling I accepted their offer for a ride out.

They let me ride with them back down the road the other way (the way I should have gone) nudged between them like they were ma and pa. I thought it was nice of them to pick-up a strange boy from the middle of nowhere. I kept looking at the shotgun and wondering things and worrying about what kind of people live in these fucking mountains. Part of me also thought that my predicament may involve taking that gun and their truck. I just wasn't that kind of person though. They too were genuinely harmless.

Traveling down winding roads and shaky earth we made small talk. I was still acting like everything was alright. They didn't want to pry or make a big deal or situation out of anything. I think they just wanted me to be safe. They mentioned the Ranch without trying to obviously implicate me. I told them that I was from there and we had been on a camping trip and I had already finished the program and was leaving now. They were kind enough to just nod their heads and humour me. In the middle of our conversation another car came speeding up the mountain and I noticed it was the course supervisor from the Ranch. I ducked lower in my seat trying not to appear obvious, but keeping an eye on him so I could see if he noticed me. He hadn't. They asked me where I was going and I said, "Wherever you are for now." They said that they were going just past town and could drop me off there. I told them that would be great.

When we stopped I acted eternally grateful and I guess I was. I shamefully asked for some money and they gave me five dollars, for which I was very grateful. In hindsight I thought, is that all you give a kid with nothing in the middle of fucking nowhere? I asked their names pointing to my head like I'd remember, so I could one day repay this gift they had given. They departed and I was left in a town that looked like an old country western film with a saloon and a convenient store. But a store had never been more convenient, where I walked proudly in with my five dollars and picked out some Doritos and a Coke. I went up to the counter where some chocolates lay. I asked the lady if they were free and she said I could have some. I flashed her my best smile and asked for more. I filled my front pouch. Outside the store was a bench I melted on. I was happy to be alive for the first time in awhile and those empty carbohydrates never tasted so good or fulfilling. After that; not too sure of what to do, I remembered my squashed pack of cigarettes and that I smoked. I walked into a novelty shop and asked the guy for a light. Some matches did the trick and I must say a cigarette was never more well deserved or enjoyed since. I sat in the New Mexico dusk feeling very calm and cool, where the air is dead and time stops. This moment could have frozen at this point for the rest of my young life. Then I started to contemplate my next move.

Connected to the store was a little gas pump unit. I saw a young woman pumping gas and I asked her if I could get a ride. She asked me where I was going. "I dunno, North East." I thought maybe I would go to Vegas where my uncle lived. She said that she was going west somewhere, I don't remember where now. "Oh, maybe next time," I replied. She smiled and was on her way. I kicked myself after she had gone, thinking of my limited options. I had nothing. How could I go away or start a new life or anything?

To my right on the store wall there was a pay phone. Unfortunately, I had to call home to state my demands and to let them know I was fine. At this point the Ranch was still choking on excuses as to why they hadn't found me yet. I picked-up the phone and made the collect call home. It went somewhat like this:

My younger brother picked-up the phone. He asked his questions and I eventually said I needed to talk to Dad.

"Hey Dad, how are ya?" I started

Aaron are you ok? where are you?" he said.

"Well ya, I guess I'm ok now. I rather not tell you exactly where I am now though I'm safe."

"How did you get there? my father wondered. "I got a ride here" I simply stated.

"I need to make sure you're alright, you need to tell me where you are so I know," he stated

"Why, so I can go back there? I'm not going back. I'm coming home for Christmas. I can get a ride home right now if I wanted," I barked.

"I know you don't like it there, if you tell me where you are I can have somebody get you and we can talk about this and arrange something."

I gave in and bought it.

After the conversation, I thought again about running, but I had already promised my dad that I wouldn't. I walked over to a small bridge and sat on the cement railing. One, so they wouldn't miss me and two, maybe to signify that I still had spirit left, what they caused me to do hadn't broken me. I sat there and waited for the cavalry to roll up and take me back to a different, but no better hell, than the mountains. It was hard to believe I went through all that just to go back, but my options were slim. I played it off as proving a point to the man.

A couple cars showed up about a half-hour later and a woman from the Ranch got out. I was expecting a lecture, but she actually gave me a big hug and thanked god I was alright. It made me feel like at least someone cared and maybe it would be okay to go back. When reaching my luxury destination I was given a rather meager meal and I got to sleep in my bed. After making the big stir I figured I would get kicked out of there soon or they would let me do what I wanted for awhile due to my traumatic experience. The next day my feet were looked after and I was given a pair of socks and told I would be taken back to the boys camp. I swore and screamed indeed that it wasn't happening. Through force and a little giving in, I ended up back at square one. You would think they would have learned.

There I was sitting back in camp, back within the mountains I worked so desperately hard to escape. I was at my wits end, sick mentally and physically. I was a textbook definition of what the Scientology dictionary calls suppressed and 'enturbulated', both meaning that I was completely worn down by a person(s) or situational factors, or in my case, both. Ironically it was due to Scientology. On a rock I wondered what to do, knowing I didn't want to spend another fucking night in these mountains sheltered by a tent or not.

Looking into the fire once again the smoke filling my eyes was an excuse to cry and not be noticed. The boys were playing their wrestling games and ignoring me. The one boy then asked me to wrestle and I told him no. They kept asking until they switched it up. They offered some cigarettes that I didn't get to have very often. The one boy asked. "What will you give me if I win?" I laughed and said my life. A joke in disguise.

We stepped in the patch of dirt to play tap out. I smiled because this kid was weak and skinny. It wasn't four seconds before I picked him off the ground. As I did, my intention was to take him down, but instead, I lost my footing or tripped over a rock. When that happened our fall was the most awkward thing ever. It's as if I blanked out and all his body weight came down on my arm. When he did my pain was instantaneous and I told him to get off I'm done. He got off and called me a pussy. Everyone walked away and left me there. I suppose not knowing or caring that I was hurt. I laid in the dirt for 30 minutes moaning in agony before one of the "counselors" came up to me. I told him my arm was broken and I couldn't get up. He could've helped me, but told me I had to do it myself. I still don't know why. I laid there until night fall and eventually picked myself up while trying to hold my arm in place as I did it. The pain was like nothing I've ever experienced before.

I marched up the hill, holding my broken arm with the other, as all the boys chilled in their tents. I went up to the counselors trailer and walked in. As I went in he asked me why I didn't knock. I was beside myself as he almost tried to put me outside.

"Have you seen my arm?" I screamed. "Aaron , you're overreacting," he returned.

"How would you know this?" I asked.

"Because you always are, you're being a baby, like always. Now get out of the trailer!"

"I'm not going anywhere, my arm is fucked. I promise you it's broken. If you don't take me to a hospital, you're going to be in a lot of fucking trouble!"

I wanted to take that gun from the holster of the one counselors to my side and waste every last motherfucker there.

Soon after, I was in a truck going to a hospital for X-Rays, in spite of their inconvenience. I've never been in that much pain and smiling. I got my wish somehow the hard way. I was taught in the readings that if a person wanted something bad enough or for long enough the mind's intention will find a way to get it. This is a universal law. The mind's intention collides with the universe and brings about the intended result. Some desires must come through hard work or passion, but always the mind is the main culprit. Anything is attainable, and might not always come by the means that was expected. There is a lesson behind any door and that's why they are all open. In this scenario, I got what I wanted, though through highly unorthodox means, it was still the only other way I was getting out of that camp aside from climbing up a mountain again and dying this time.

The next thing I remember was getting a shot of Demerol and waking up to a nurse and a doctor pulling my arm back into place. I asked them what the hell they were doing and they told me. I passed-out again and woke-up soon after asking if we were getting our allowance tonight in a confused state. The allowance I was supposed to receive every week, but rarely saw for some reason. The counselors who were still there laughed. I smiled and lost consciousness again.

I got McDonald's that night and my own bed in a motel. I couldn't be happier, as this felt like an achievement. I woke up the next morning bright eyed and excited to see T.V for the first time really in a month and a half. I laughed away watching Crocodile Dundee on cable. We then went out to breakfast and I kept on saying that my parents would pay them back for this out of my gratitude. They probably just took it out of my parents deposit anyway, along with the other monies that weren't being extracted for my general needs.

I was then taken back to the Ranch and the boys were back from an excursion. They continued to cut me off from everyone else by putting me back in the home camp. I spent all day near this rundown little trailer where the boys would come by and prey on my weakness, picking fights with me and still tipping over the outhouse, flipping me over on my arm. I hadn't slept since I got back there and was ill. I still had fight in me, but I wasn't thinking right. The trailer outside was cold and I didn't have proper warmth. I never asked anyone for anything, not being sure that they would've given me anything, but I just as soon stay awake all night inside by the fire since they were asleep. I didn't think I needed sleep and my body couldn't have agreed more.

More time passed and I got the call up to the Executive Directors office. I was told that my mother was coming here to check in on me. They made out like I wasn't going home that she was just visiting. I was excited to see her, but Christmas was soon upon its way and I was confused whether to stay and wait for her. I didn't want to spend the holidays here, even with her. I wanted to be home, so as she left on a plane to come here, I started to pack some yogurt and fruit in a backpack and left on foot for home. I also packed the only thing that was of significance to me here, which was a rock I found on the Ranch that crumbled down from the mountains. In the middle of the rock was a white colored heart, the type of shape young girls use to dot their "i"s with. It symbolized hope for me and maybe love when I got back home.

This time I stuck to the road hoping I left at the right time as to not draw detection for awhile. The road was a long valley road with only one way out, and there were no cutoffs for escape. I walked this road the good part of the morning and tried to stay in the ditch to the side, so I would not be obvious despite my bright yellow jacket. Every so often when a car came I would think about coming out of the ditch to hitchhike but then decide against it, not sure if I was doing the right thing. Eventually a car pulled up to me and stopped, and sure enough it was some of the counselors. They didn't say much to get me in the car. I didn't put up a fight; I wasn't even sure what I was doing anymore. I was emotionally spent and gone.

The next few days I waited eagerly for my mom to arrive. I missed her and maybe she would see that there was something going on other than my behavioral problems. Over the 36 hours of waiting, I tried to decide whether I would leave with her or if I would stay here another year to finish this program. The anxiety was really over having to escape again for I would not ever be finishing anything by their rules. I wasn't sure I could trust her to make the right decision for me. I thought it was likely they would tell her lies about me and change things up during her stay.

The day would come and she would be here. I waited all day in my still assigned area. As another dark night fell, a spark in my eyes flickered as she arrived. I ran up to meet her where she was already inside. I experienced mixed emotions when I saw her. It was hard to not have anger for being put here, and the trust I had in her to always have my best interests in mind had been shaken. I gave her a big hug and gave her the benefit of the doubt for that second's embrace. She could tell something was wrong right away by my crazed, glazed over, enlarged pupils, and rough looking facial hair that had never before existed on me. I was dirty and had no shoes on. I had remembered walking through dirt and gravel to see her but I don't remember doing it with no shoes. She was overwhelmed at the sight of me.

It didn't take long before she was on the phone with my father to tell that we would be coming home. After a short visit with my mom, three men came and tried to put me back in the trailer to sleep. I fought with them and said that I wasn't. My mom came out and told them that the program was over for me and I'd be staying with her in the room they gave her. It would be another 6 days before they could or would arrange a ride for us to the airport.

Before we left, my mom consulted the powers that be as to where my clothes had gone. I had come with new clothes and now there were none left. The cunt director pleaded ignorance and blamed it on me, calling me a psych case as they do in Scientology. She had said that I was smart but too smart for my own good, whatever that meant. This negative woman and these people had the audacity to call themselves Scientologists and to judge people. My mother told her that I may be sick right now, but I wasn't like these boys and that I didn't belong here. The woman did agree that I didn't belong here, but not in that regard. My mother went on to bark at her about how misguided her description of this place was and how they ran the camp like a prison. Disappointment was not the word to describe this situation. To date they still owe us thousands, but has since been closed down.

My sacred disc-man was in the hands of another boy after a month had passed and I was still here. He took it when I wasn't looking and hid it. My mom demanded it back and the mother of the boy said that it was obtained through a bet. Some of the boys' parents worked here so it was no surprise they were without ethics as well. My mom told her to get it back from her son by the time we left.

That night, my mother was walking back to her room when a boy stopped her and started a brief conversation. He said to her, that it wasn't right the way they had treated me. As she was ready to respond, the other director, a big scary bear of a man, came from around the corner and asked is if everything was okay, trying to secure his investment in this dump. The boy answered yes and was on his way quickly to avoid a reprimand.

The next day I was up earlier than usual, as I was hardly able to contain my excitement about leaving and getting on a plane. I laid in the dark and played the Eurythmics, waiting for six in the morning to come. In the airport I was erratic, being with my mother and then gone like a child. When it was time to board the plane, I was off having a conversation with an American girl, and just taking in the freedom. Eventually, when we got on the plane, my high strung ways posed to be too much for my mother, so she slipped some Ativan (an anti-depressant) into my soda to get me us through the trip. This was against my previous psychiatrist's orders and the church's, but she knew I needed rest.

ChapTer sixTeen

I got my wish and was home for Christmas. My face was lit up like a tree for the holidays, especially when I walked into the church and was greeted by two sexy young French Canadian Scientologists. They were both members of the Sea Organization, the core sect in Scientology where these people devote their lives to people's "freedom" through the spread of the religion. The first girl, I already knew because she studied at the church where she worked in a cramped room for little a day. She was away from home, living out a billion year contract, literally, which they ask their workers to sign in order to show devotion to humanity. It symbolizes dedication in not only this life, but many more to come for this cause. Of course this contract isn't legally binding and is more of an ethical as well as a moral obligation. This is the moral fiber that Scientologists are supposed to be infested with.

The other girl was a very attractive young woman who was also there with an older woman from the same establishment. They had come to check up on our city's church, to improve stats, and to try to talk my father into becoming its executive director. My father had money and intelligence and was the only person for the job, considering our membership didn't exceed twenty. When they started to take me out with them, I had little lunches together with the cute one and I didn't question it, I just enjoyed the time. We would go out for food, and she and I would talk. I'd make out like we were getting hot and heavy, having two dates in one day as a joke. She would scold me jokingly, assuring me this wasn't what it was. I still don't know if she was there partly to calm me down or if she enjoyed my company. We, along with her partner would all go out to little night spots in town to see live bands play. Being the way I was, I had no apprehension getting up and singing, and even intruding upon a set to sing back up for someone. They told me I was great and stroked my manic ego.

Around this time I went to live with the teen counselor in Toronto again. Things slipped quickly between her and I. She felt that I had changed. Undetectable to me, my experience at the Ranch may have hardened me to some point and my attitude may have stiffened. Losing a pinch of my innocence our relationship suffered. I was smoking now, which put a damper on our whole athletic regime we had going. She didn't like that. When cleaning out my room she would expose my porno magazines just to embarrass me, a dirty secret to be respected among young men.

Things started to go even worse and we were having arguments all the time. I was supposed to be looking for a job and wasn't really. I was still going to modeling interviews to get out of real work. I got a girlfriend at the movies. Her friend phoned me and set it up and before I had the chance to kiss her, two days later I left the place due to the tension. This tension existed solely because of me; even though we were paying her, she owed my parents through borrowing from them – they were trying to keep a fellow Scientologist afloat so she could help me. Not only did she owe my parents money and couldn't pay them back, she also had a side job of stealing Scientology educational data to teach children. We had outgrown each other and I had lost another friend. It was onto the next phase.

So easy to deny are wrongs, And to enjoy our
songs.
Was it me or was it you?
Hurt is more real than happiness.
Rejection the root of sadness. Was it me or was
it you?
How many times did I not notice I was liked.
My memory becomes flawless of every thorn
in my side.
I knew when it was you.
How many times was it me?

The friendship fizzled-out and my stay had been drawn-out. She owed my parents a substantial amount of money. That wasn't the issue for them of course. They had to figure out what to do with me; not to get rid of me, but to find an answer to my erratic behavior and overall sketchiness. So, when my father picked me up after that weekend, he had another proposal for me.

This time the offer was to go to Oklahoma to a treatment centre called Narconon. The Sea-Org woman who came down had convinced my father that this was the best thing to do. I was considered an illegal pre-clear because of my short stint on anti-depressants. A pre-clear is the beginning of the Scientology food chain ladder I mentioned before. I was illegal because I had taken psychiatric drugs. My mother had taken verbal abuse from members over time for letting me do this. However, if psychiatric drugs are administered by family doctors its ok with the church for some reason. I would be unable to climb the ladder unless I was involved in a drug detoxification course. It would involve basic exercise, vitamins and sauna, along with Scientology education again. But I couldn't do it at any ordinary church because I was illegal. It had to be done at a safe place where everyone was a risk you could say. Yet no one on street drugs is deemed illegal, although they are worse, mind-altering intoxicants. This is the rationalization.

I'm not sure why all religions have contradictions, but all of them seem to. Maybe it's because religions cannot be perfect, or maybe they were and got changed around to orchestrate confusion to keep people ignorant. Or it could be a plan for fear-mechanism propaganda that exists in any group used for indoctrination and conditioning. My own belief being as strong as it was, I was apt to defend Scientology's name not too long ago. Then I would catch myself and think it's silly, and then turn around and question that. No one in Scientology brainwashed me. They didn't get a chance to, since I was an open-minded prime candidate for self involvement at the time. Scientology itself can manipulate anyone interested.

Again, I was given the spiel that I could get away. This time it would be different and I would have fun. I was told that it wasn't a boot camp of any kind. This place would appreciate me and it was a way to get me on my way up the Scientology Bridge. This was ridiculous because I knew more than most Scientologists who were higher up than me. Illegal or not I already felt higher up the plain then someone who had maybe spent more money on auditing. But I was ill, no question about that, and I agreed to the trip again. What did I care? I wasn't doing anything really. My mother told everyone it wasn't a good idea. She spoke with the directors in Oklahoma telling them that I wasn't healthy enough for this and asking if they were prepared for lashing out and possibly suicide attempts. She felt strongly that this was just too much, but she was overpowered by the church and my father. My parents both had my best interests in mind, but I'm not sure that the church did. Perhaps they viewed Narconon as another source to get me out of the way. Since I was in the most part what some people in the church who didn't know me but knew of me, would call a DB. This being a phrase in Scientology meaning a degraded-being. A term sometimes thrown around too loosely when a Scientologist becomes grandiose in thinking and decides to judge others. I have never realized the audacity of some of these "big wigs" in the Toronto church. To call me a bad seed before meeting me and to tell my mother to accept it in the interest of my situation and the church to not cloud my parents judgment. I'm sure no one called L Ron Hubbard's son Quentin Hubbard a DB for being a homosexual and killing himself in 1976. Scientology is different from other religions but it also considers homosexuality an aberration in some of the texts like Dianetics. L Ron Hubbard wrote this himself. The rationalization behind it was that people are individuals and sometimes have no link to the parents and there is no help for them. They couldn't tell my parents to give up on me but it was implied by certain Scientologists. My parents believed we are connected for a reason and I wasn't choosing to act out deep down.

ChapTer SevenTeen

I was taking all of these trips, but I didn't feel like I had done anything wrong. I didn't feel like the church had rejected me and I didn't feel that my parents were disappointed. There was no reason, everyone close to me just wanted to help but they were being told what to do by people who didn't and only cared about the interests of the religion. I felt great and from what I knew about karma, good will et cetera, I could not feel this way unless I was a good person doing good things. I wasn't taking being sent off as a bad thing, but instead as something being done to help me out of love. This was the journey I had to take. Even if the actions along the way were extreme, I didn't know how to be anyone other than myself. The person I had accepted was the person I was now. Everything wasn't explained to me and most of the time I was in a state of mild to high elation where I felt good, hell everything felt good and I rolled with it. It was hard to not buy this confidence as legitimate since I could not be brought down for months and months on end. This feeling was something I believed could be possible in the religion, however due to my questionable state over the past couple years, it made it made the "Scientology effect" embellished even more.

I sat there again and I was excited to be where I was - amongst a lot of drug-addicts introducing myself. Having only touched marijuana a handful of times, I stood up and said my name and location as everyone gasped, as if to say how fucked up is he being shipped all the way down here? It definitely felt different, and people were friendly and they were finding hope in their lives again, which is always a rejuvenation of the soul and surroundings. Optimism seemed to be in the air. Oklahoma, as I was beginning to feel, was full of fresh new breezes.

That same night my father left, sending me out once more as a sheep amongst wolves. After the introductions, I was taken to the detox/withdrawal house, a small stone home on the grounds to spend as long as it took to get over the initial jitters away from the population. This was where the withdrawal process began and ended and there was someone on watch all night. I, of course didn't have this to conquer. However, I did have to deal with a gorgeous young girl giving me a massage before bed. In Scientology this was called a nerve assist to relax someone and realign and calm the nerves. I had never seen a Scientologist that beautiful and thought I was in heaven. When she turned me over to massage my front she got a surprise. She had a subtle smile after she had noticed, but wasn't trying to make it noticeable. I went to sleep embarrassed and aroused. I would find out later that she was an ex-Vegas show girl and a drug addict. Scientologists didn't look like that, not where I was from anyway and apparently not here either.

Settling in, people were kind to me and there were attractive women on the grounds. I started in on a course just like I had before at home and at the ranch. Before I had started, the course supervisor started asking me questions about my history.

"So what are you here for? Coke? He asked. "No" I responded.

"Crack?" "No"

"Heroin?"

"No," I said again. "Meth?"

"No, I'm uh just here. I was sent here for Scientology. Isn't it in my file?"

I wasn't sure what to say. He shrugged it off, accepting that maybe I didn't want to say, since no one had ever been there for not doing drugs. I had to go through and pass the rudimentary courses to go through to be ready for the purification. They wanted the mind to be stable first. I wouldn't say my mind was stable, but I was the only person there who had already had a history of the education. I welcomed the challenge, and it was a cinch. My mind had been working overtime for a long time now and it would not die out. The anticipation of being in a new place made it more stimulating. In this security my mind had calmed for the time being. I was tested on books I read to make absolutely sure I understood; I was asked to define words one after another at random and I responded with no pause or delay. What I liked about Scientology was the act of becoming literate without the illusion that you know what a word means as we so vaguely and often do. I wasn't judged inside a course room and graded like in school, I was praised and it made me work harder. I believed my IQ was immensely shooting up, maybe it was, but combined with my mind's inability to shut down, I was wired and always thinking which can also be an illusion of intelligence. I was the only person there still on a high. It was after the testing that the rest of the people in the room took a second away from their books to say that I did a good job and they were impressed with my knowledge of the English language. I felt a calling if I hadn't already. I wanted to be a Scientology master. I wanted to save myself and the world and I would be the leader of this movement.

In that week I spent more time doing some routines that I had already done before. The first was completing the exercise of sitting across from someone for an hour with eyes closed, as I'd done before. Again this was to increase confront levels in communication and to put us back in touch with our surroundings. This time, the course room supervisor was a hot blond and at 55 minutes she flunked me. That meant you had to start from the beginning. She said I was showing somatics, which meant a body reaction or twitch due to the mind trailing off. Really I was almost falling asleep. I wanted to put off a casual vibe towards her because of my attraction, but I went up to her and said it was bullshit and I stormed out. I was calm, but I lost it in a moment when I could hardly contain myself, as had been the problem for some time now. I could not have anyone question me.

I walked back to the building where we stayed and started watching T.V. with some of the guys. Sitting there in anger, one of the girls I had noticed before came up to me and I realized she was sent to get me back. She too was coincidentally beautiful or I was really in need of a female touch. This time-frame was blurry, but when she spoke I listened and the anger subsided. With her soft gentle voice and her red hair like a flame, she lit a torch. I was back in the course room doing what I had to on the outside, but burning for her on the inside.

As the days went on the meals were superb, being cooked by professionals, not like the slop at the ranch. People were usually nice and I made a few friends my own age. We would play volleyball and basketball, and ping-pong became a regular and fun thing. Every night before bed I would read L Ron Hubbard's calming words and settle myself to sleep sometimes. As I would walk to breakfast I would always pass that girl walking the opposite way. I would wave or gesture trying to get her to notice me. Life there was becoming content and actually enjoyable. It was like a small village cut-off from the rest of the world. I was not missing home a bit.

The place had many successful people within it. I suppose this made sense being they could afford the treatment and the drugs it took to get there. There was a pro-surfer, an ex-boxer, a doctor, a few entrepreneurs and others. I felt like I could look up to these people. They had problems that I never felt could confiscate my life, but I didn't even have a life yet and these people had been places and done things and were able, aside from their afflictions. I thought we could both offer each other knowledge. I wanted them to like me.

I socialized with the people there. For the first time in my life I was interested in others pasts and what they had to say. I still needed my somewhat inflated amount of alone time and every once and a while I would wonder a bit too far off the premises as I had before. We were supposed to stay on the grounds, but I would go further just for a different view and get talked to later when I would shrug them off. Most of the time, it was enough for me to just be there. I hadn't ever felt so free in such a confined space and my quarters were just a bedroom. I had heard the place was built on an old Indian burial ground. I could swear I felt it somehow. It was different here, the fog and the wind felt like walking through a never ending dream. Early on, I began to feel that there was something mystical and unearthly about this place. This felt like freedom for the first time ever, even though the financial support of my parents remained. Nonetheless, I felt like a cloud. Somehow everything I needed was here now.

ChapTer eighTeen

As time passed, new people came. I was excited for every new soul to come through the doors into a new life. I was getting to a point of accepting anyone who was getting on the path towards Scientology freedom because we needed all the support we could get. Everyone who came through, however, had promise and something to offer which was more exciting. I never met a plain old crack head there. Everyone was just so special, it seemed. My emotions were changing too. And then there was the red head, my eyes collapsing on her every time I thought she wasn't noticing. When she did, I'd look away just late enough so she wouldn't notice I was looking. She was heaven sent and there for me.

I had heard from someone that it was her birthday coming up. I took advantage of this information by getting her a card and writing her a poem. I actually mustered up the balls to give it to her and to pull her away from a conversation to do it. I still didn't know how to talk to girls and the poem probably wasn't much better, very indirect about my feelings. She acknowledged it very maturely and was appreciative for it. I wasn't sure how much older she was than me at the time. Finding out later that she used to be a hooker made things a bit strange and soured the appeal a little, but not fully by any means for some reason. I wasn't sure what was more disappointing, that my poem seemed to get me nowhere, or that she used to trick. Like anything then, it slid off my back and I went on to the next thing.

After my attention was off of her a little bit, it was projected more intensely onto other things. Another let down just meant pouring myself into the only thing that would save me in the end anyway, which were his words. I studied harder and worked harder. I was starting again to live in his world. I would begin to press my opinions on people. When I felt I knew more, the more I felt I was getting stronger. That is what I was told Scientology did. I suppose to a point. Knowledge can make you stronger but sometimes I would start to act ignorant like I had no care, and that life was beautiful, Mr. Rogers bullshit. However, not being that sort of person innately. I wasn't any kind of person anymore. My identity was fleeting, caught up in whatever emotion my mind chose to latch on to at that moment. A roller coaster that you're not aware you're on.

I had heard earlier that some women there will fake that they locked themselves out of their room to get you to go over to them. They will then initiate sex. Once I was walking out the lobby door of our quarters when a woman in just a towel said she locked herself out. (I however had no lock on my door and never noticed until now - this had to be because of what my mom told them). I asked her what she wanted me to do. She didn't really respond. I told her I'll get someone and as she was saying no, I was already walking out. I told someone and he gave me a funny look and then I realized after thinking about, what she wanted. That was another missed chance to reach manhood, but one I could have done without, as I didn't go back over.

There always seemed to be something going on. I was never bored there. When I was, my mind thought of things to do because it was overactive. Each day, I started to sleep less and less again. Every night I spent a little more time obsessing about my future and my reason for being here.

I listened to aggressive music and acted out music videos physically, until I drained myself into a few hours of sleep. A healthy mind can be creative when it chooses to and knows when to cease. An ill mind doesn't know and can't grasp the value of either until the difference between creative and irrational are all lost.

I would escape to talk to the horses again, they had on the grounds. They would look at me in understanding of the ideas that most humans didn't want to understand. I would sing to them too and comfort them in the way I was comforted by my reassurance of what I knew. I know now who was comforting who.

My time there started to be like college dorms without the drinking, something I would never experience being a Scientologist. There would be late nights talking with some ex-junkies and learning about the streets a little bit. Sometimes I would give my far out opinions about life, past lives, other planets, and aliens - my views either through Scientology, hearsay, or of my own accord. For people who deep down couldn't give a shit about Scientology, they were very open and accepting, far more than regular people. We would get into philosophical ramblings in which I was starting to take seriously and the conversation was referred to as like an acid trip for them. We would laugh and everyone got along. Sometimes I would just sit and listen to stories about drugs all night until my head spun from a lack of reality as we called it, or personal experience. (This doesn't exist, but reading about "lack of reality" in Scientology made my head fuzzy because I believed it). The boys introduced me to The Dave Mathews Band who were popular amongst college students at the time in the U.S. I felt like I was in the higher education and had mature friends for the first time.

Eventually another shipment of newbie's had arrived and I made a close new friend with one of them. He was a quiet, passive and intelligent guy. I remember that. We seemed to compliment each other. My ways of speech were starting to change at this point. I started to question people because I wanted to make them answer their own problems without me saying it. This way they taught themselves. He asked me one time if I knew I spoke in riddles. I played dumb, upset that he was on to me. We would laugh and carry on together and things were looking up for us. It was around then that I would start the actual purification/ detoxification rundown.

ChapTer nineTeen

We started in the morning, at breakfast. We would then take our vitamins consisting of niacin to get the radiation out. From there we would do our exercise for at least 40 minutes. Lastly we would go in the sauna for 20 to 30 minutes. I basically had the rest of the day to myself after that. That wasn't necessarily a good thing, since I was becoming more obsessed with myself.

With each passing day I felt like I was getting stronger and that my body was catching up with my mind. I'd be invincible. Every morning for exercise I would work the heavy bag that belonged to the ex-boxer who stayed there. He would watch me and comment on my fighting skills. I would start to go off on the bag and it would eventually fall off the hinges. It was a bit loose to begin with. He would say that's okay, just come and tell me when it happens. I kept going crazy on the bag and knocking it down and I would forget and to tell him to the point where he was getting pissed.

In general, I was starting to disregard other's opinions and demands. My kindness was starting to turn into aggressiveness. When bigger guys who used to pick on me a little bit said something now, I would lash out at them with a twitch of my eyes. When they got physical, I became more physical as well, until they didn't want to pick on me anymore. I was becoming something not to be reckoned with.

I don't know what it was, but I'm pretty sure I did at the time. I deserved respect for the first time in my life. Even before someone becomes something they must act the part beforehand to get it. There was no control or idea for an outcome.

From here on the days began to morph together. It was a week or two of one long fairytale from my perspective. One long nightmare, if I was actually able to see myself and analyze my feelings. What led up to the following came quickly and without warning. I speculate that these events will not be told in full detail or correct order, but only in a full memory of what is, remembered and what was seen....

I was practicing my religious studies in my room and the information was becoming more real and meaningful to me. The mixture of illness (whatever it was) and education were coming together. In Scientology when we understand something we become more aware and can feel it. As if an actual light bulb switching on in our heads, we become more "there" and our tone goes up. This confirms that it is true. There are also different levels of understanding. I was under the influence of believing I understood the words fully for the first time. We were taught that things take on different meanings as we mature. The fact that my mind would blast in and out with the illusion of superior consciousness would only verify it for me. At this point there was no way to tell the difference since it was me choosing to have realizations rather than them happening naturally, which is becoming increasingly clear what founded Scientology, the desperation and the desire to feel wise to the point of fooling themselves. Not only here, but anywhere group indoctrination is practiced to "educate" people. The people who can't learn through pure intelligence or life experience are subjected to this always or until they finally have an awakening. Most who ever had a "divine affirmation" or a "God-sent vision" needed to in order for them to be right. Oh what the mind can see if the body has no reason to live without it. You cannot blame the sheep. The herdsman is always looked past since most are afraid to question someone who is fully aware of what he is doing for good or evil. I stumbled across the L Ron axiom, "time is a consideration," and something clicked. It was as though I understood it and this was a missing piece to my serenity. The quote just at the time was most likely understood as something else and taken too literally. I held my alarm clock up to my face and examined its falseness as though it had weighed me down my entire life. I then proceeded to punch through the plastic and then I kung-fu kicked it out my window since I had no need for time anymore. I stared at the blood on my hand as a needful sacrifice for my newfound affirmation.

I sat and hung from my window sill with the cool breeze stroking my bloody hand, mystified by the moon light glaring out the window. The light from the moon wasn't keeping me up since I had been awake for at least four days straight now, but the light was keeping me interested. I looked out of my third story window with my legs dangling further, strangely because I had always been afraid of heights, but nothing lately or for a long time now was as it were. Hanging there, I contemplated more personal long-drawn out theories involving self-improvement, ethics, past and future lives and the idea that they might have been lived on other planets (a sort of underground theory of Scientology that previous lives were lived elsewhere). Some of us were apparently sent here because we did not comply and follow rules. So earth being the place we were sent to do what we wanted and suffer the consequences and fend for ourselves.

Not out of hallucination yet I believe, but at this point a coincidence I saw what I genuinely believed to be a U.F.O. This object was hovering at a nearby distance over a cattle field, which I thought gave credit to my vision. What I thought was a craft was moving at a slow pace not towards me but to the left. My glare turned into a glaze. There were faint lights around the craft. They were white and red and flashing, it seemed to be rotating subtly. Not with fear but utter amazement I beamed in on this. I could see cars in the distance and I could see that there was no comparison. The subject had always been of keen interest and this interest during this night kept getting fiercer. It could be easy to conceive that this was just a delusion in my compromised state that fed personal fantasy. Maybe a coincidental inconvenience to make my mental state worse and more confused. Though even I cannot trust my judgment as it was disappearing into a sky of unidentifiable measures itself.

I ran downstairs to get a closer look at the craft. I had planned to run right underneath it, greet them and maybe join them. At least long enough to learn their advanced knowledge, like what I thought L Ron Hubbard knew. I could come back and enlighten my fellow man. As I ran downstairs I caught the eye of the night security man, who I think had already had been told to watch me closely. When I came, I told him to follow me loudly and he trailed behind. I sped around the front corner of the building to where it had been only to see nothing now. I explained to him that it was right there a few minutes ago. The man humored me, but with him being previously notified about my behavior, I don't think he wanted to escalate matters by showing me doubt, especially judging by the size of my pupils.

Going back up to my room I was a little embarrassed and very disappointed. I saw it and it had existed. The rest of the night was spent obsessing about it. The nights were becoming endless and when I couldn't read or listen to music, I would philosophize and put an interpretive spin on everything to the point of distortion. Thoughts would get confused and these thoughts would have to be worked out to rational conclusions in my head, even if it took all night. Sometimes the thoughts would keep coming and invalidate or contradict my original conclusion and I would have to start over to work it out.

A few days later I was relaxing in the hall where we ate. Sitting very strange and observing people as they did what they do. I remember having an all-knowing demeanor about me and when a guy I knew saw me he said, "Hey you, what are you up to? I know you're up to something." I didn't know exactly what it was, however I knew it was something. I wasn't sure how he knew and I'm not sure I liked him knowing. I'm not sure he meant anything by it. I just gave him a coy smile of assurance. I assumed the smile indicated that he not tell anyone. If he knew what I was doing then he would understand because he would have to read my mind to. I started to consider him for my mission, even though this mission didn't really exist and my plans were actually meaningless thoughts.

I don't know how long this dream lasted, whether it was a week or two weeks. I remember stepping inside the fence with the horses and they followed me, both of them followed me and a straight line as I sang to them. I didn't know if this was normal, but it was euphoric. At a Friday night graduation I came in while a man was giving his speech for a course completed. I'd remembered he had a stutter, so I put my head in my lap and concentrated as I waved my hand exactly like a conductor, making his speech flow along. I didn't hear him stutter the whole time and I knew I caused that.

On this day it started snowing, which was rare for Oklahoma in general I suppose, but especially at this time. It came down quick upon the soil that was still warm. As the residents started to play in it, I stood from the kitchen window embracing this moment as the first time I had created snow. "Dance my children, dance," I muttered under my breath. "Enjoy it while it lasts." I watched them have fun, as I basked in the glory I created for them. The snow hailed down and this being the reason by where I hailed from. I stepped outside and watched them as they lived so care free. The snow was my influence from Canada and I thought of it as a present from me to them for their hard work here. Also, a good time before the real work I had for them would begin.

ChapTer TwenTy

My door now had no knob. It didn't occur to me that there was surveillance going on...I was just concerned about having no door knob. I peeked through the hole to make sure it wasn't there. Soon after, I found the maintenance guy on my same floor. A big 6"5 guy weighing about 270 at least. I shouted at him and motioned him to come over. I asked violently if he took off the door knob. He responded "Yes," And when I asked why he started to stutter. Under normal conditions, I would have been surprised that I had made a man this big afraid. I then asked him where the door knob was, and as I was impatient already, I was off to find it. I went straight downstairs as if I knew where it was. I saw a plastic bag on a table and ripped into it revealing the knob. Running back upstairs I threw it to him and told him to put it back on.

Later that night I walked downstairs again from my room. I sat relaxed but not too much on the couch where a college basketball game was on. I started to enjoy myself as I had gotten away from things I liked lately. It came down to the wire at the end of the game and I started to smile as if I knew what was going to happen. There was nine seconds left and the one team put up an unlikely three-ball to tie the game. Before it went in I pointed to the T.V. with a gesture of my finger to put it in and the ball went down. I started to laugh, knowing what I did. Then with five seconds left the opposing team ran the ball up court and had to throw up a shot from at least 35 feet away that had no chance. I raised my finger and motioned the ball in by moving my finger towards the net. When that sank I laughed hard in delight but not surprise. Some others were just staring at me I thought in amazement at what I did. Of course it was a strange coincidence with a strange character. Occurrences like this were only feeding my illusion of power. Something as strange as watching a basketball game in your head on television other than the one going on, is out of our grasp. Who knew that you could control hallucinations?

The hallucinations came out of nowhere but when they did, I considered it, finally my upwards state of being as Scientology claims to give. That is the genius of this brainwashing technique

-- there is always a quote to give hope to your frustration and that leads you to delusion at which point you will accept anything. This fact doesn't exactly apply to me however because I wasn't deluded, I never accepted any information that didn't make sense I was merely on the verge of insanity with the fanatic ramblings of Scientology, which made my trip quicker and more involved.

When I walked out of the dark T.V. room into the light, everyone's face looked different than minutes earlier. I had always seen people as ordinary; they were nothing special, just another person. But that night I came into a foyer full of people and saw love. I sat with some guys who were playing cards and their faces were lit up. Every feature was flawless and every nice characteristic was accentuated. People were passing and I would tell them that they looked good. They would smile in embarrassment. Everybody was beautiful. I had been working up to being something and this is what it was. I was witnessing human beings through our idea of God's eyes and it was miraculous. It seemed as though I was seeing people as they would look in heaven. I remember still the perfectness, for a brief second seeing everyone's soul on the outside. I was just staring at people and they were starting to wonder what was wrong, or maybe what could be so right.

This stream of events will never be able to be fully explained for me. It seemed apparent that on my way to this psychosis my mind was choosing to carry out my fantasies, a desire for power, knowledge and control, at least over my own life. My desires were stronger than most people's because of my drive and condition. I have wondered if at one point my brain was imbalanced so much that another part of it was actually functioning at a higher percentage. That because my brain had not been turned off for so long, the circuitry had been pushed to the outer limits just before breakdown. It is possible that my brain was overcompensating for a lack somewhere else and picking up on untouched waters in other areas. It wasn't that I was controlling anything, but it seemed as if I knew things that were happening before they did and seeing things we weren't meant to. The unreality of these events only sheds light on the reality of insanity. It's still hard to admit that none of it was real because some of the feelings felt right although they were unnatural to me, but right. If anything, they were a sign to not give up on the journey of the advancement of the spirit..

There is not a lot of documentation on this type of phenomenon, because at this high point the crash comes soon after and leaves little evidence. As to the validity of the brain functioning at a higher and foreign level, it would be hard to confirm or deny because of how little we know. There haven't been many studied or recalled cases, but have been some studies supporting this. My illness could have been leading me to desperate fantasies. Things could be said to feel more real when you're crazy, because everything is so foreign and drastic. People told me I was finishing their sentences before they told me what they were going to say.

Look no further, And we go no further.
We're concerned with our past even though its nothingness.
We can't move on if we remember.
Nor if we forget.
To have an ending there must be a start.
To move on we filter out the bad.
Even when I try I can't retrieve all I've had.
To the point that some fixate the brain swells.
Just before breakdown the mind serves us well.

What came next was a slew of encounters and episodes. The night after was the kind of night that passes you by, but you are not aware you are living it. It was a weekend night on a Friday and we let loose a little. I hung out with my friend whose name I regretfully can't remember. It was a strange day due to the way I was acting and we had a black out for a long period, which I was sure that my energy had consumed and caused. We went around from room to room observing and chatting with the older guys until eventually making it back to his room where we lay on his bed and listened to tunes. He had neon lights in his room which made it trance like, but not the kind where you're conscious, but where your eyes are fixed and you're dead inside. As he passed out I left to roam around more.

Upon making my way back around to his room I passed it to go to the washroom. On my way I passed the steps and saw my friend sitting on the top of the stairwell. As I passed, he turned his head to the side to acknowledge someone walking by. I didn't say anything because it was as if I knew that he was exteriorized from his body. All I was seeing was his spirit and at the time I knew this. That's why I didn't say anything; I thought it rude to talk to a spirit when I could just go wake him up. He was clear, see through but whole. When I came back he was gone from the stairs and this didn't faze me. He was in his bedroom the whole time. It's a fair assumption that my fantasies were coming out through my sickness. To no avail or surprise of my own these visions and thoughts had no toll on me emotionally. Until tomorrow.

I had never seen a day that bright before with the snow still on the ground and the Oklahoma sun penetrating every crystal, blinding me through every cylinder. I felt sad today, as all the energy is built up for a crash. I walked into the hall being careful to only step on the colored square tiles. Walking forward I focused in on a couple arm in arm and with every step my mind would tell me, "look at them, they're happy" colored tile, " they're in love", "you'll never find love" colored tile. I looked down then up again. "No one will love you! You're not okay, no one could ever love you Aaron!!"

With that I hurled myself off the sequence of floor tiles and into chaos. Shoulder first I went into the wall six feet to my left and yelped. I cried and balled the most heartfelt cry I had ever felt even if it was not based on reality. I felt this emotional pain throughout every inch of my body. As though everything I had seen and couldn't handle, every sleepless night, every insecurity came crashing down on me. I was letting out two years full of pent up aggression and regression. Whatever my ailment, it hadn't allowed me to show any kind of weakness or rational thought to deter me. Whatever I had avoided was starting to crash into my awareness in split second assaults, one after another. A woman came to my rescue as I was twitching and panicking on the floor. She got me to my feet and took me out of there.

She led me aside and did some of the assists on me. I had started to feel better. Their thoughts were that if they could just get me through this detox I would be fine and it was the toxins being run out that was doing this to me.

That evening I sat down with some of the counselors to eat dinner. They weren't about to segregate me yet. I seemed fine again, quiet. During dinner my eyes narrowed because I realized I had heard that the guy next to me (who was one of the nicest guys I do recall) was dating the red headed girl that I had decided I still liked. I rose from my chair and actually pointed my finger at him and yelled out in a deep throated gibberish as if to call a duel like in the old days. I kept threatening as the counselors got me into a neutral area again as I let them. The rest of the day is vague and blurry until later when I started putting coat hangers on everyone's door knobs who would be spared in my revolution. That was my thinking, though there was a hanger on pretty much every knob when I was finished except mine. There was still no doorknob there. I then started sneaking into people's rooms and hiding their clocks. I went to the main halls and rooms and hid the clocks there too. When I got bored I would put them back up then hid them again. It got to a point where people started to notice, and the ex-boxer had caught me and he called me over. He was already pissed about me knocking over his heavy bag for the third time and wanted to rip into me a bit. He told me to give him the clock and he put his hand on it. I said no and pulled back and this went on for a few minutes. I threw his hand sideway's and let go of the clock. People were around and gasping, watching me stand up to this tough Italian with eyes that were ready to go rounds.

No one knew what was happening. I was a normal person just a week ago; even I had a better idea of my mental instability then anyone else, until now. No one expected this, even being forewarned by earlier behavior. I was gathered to a room by a few people to talk to my parents. The phone call was made and assumed this wasn't the first time in the past couple days that they were phoned concerning my condition. I smiled in joy and was happy to speak to them. I explained that I was L Ron Hubbard's confidant in my past life and that my prior knowledge was coming back to me here in this life. (The counselors were amazed at how much intricate Scientology data I was spewing, my swelled brain was tapping into everything I'd ever read somehow). I told them that I was in the tone 22.0 of the tone scale. This is a very high tone level meaning the act of controlling the game of life and winning. In my instance I was merely taking Scientology information and "glibly" relating it to children's games in an adult setting. I don't remember anything my mother or father said. I doubt I was listening because my brain couldn't receive anything. There was too much in there trapped and outgoing. When the receiver dropped, so did my memories of at least the next 12 hours.

Fast forwarding to the next day, I remember being unusually fatigued as if I had been slipped something, but most likely my mind had shut down from stress. I was crawling into a bed that wasn't mine. Before I was put to bed someone asked me if I needed something and I said a pack of Marlboros. I then closed my eyes and dreamt thoughts that were no longer mine anymore. From pure exhaustion, I slept until early evening. I didn't receive any cigarettes and had in fact already forgotten my addiction, but someone gave me a paint set and I started to doodle with that. One helper asked me what my sign meant and I told him it was peace in Chinese. He gave me a face showing either doubt or surprise.

I was officially under a Scientology type 3 watch, which involved full supervision over a person who is a threat to mostly him or her self. From now on I was to stay here and there was always at least two people outside my always opened door, watching me. Everything from this point on I related to something else. I was confident that I had all the secret information of Scientology and bad people would turn up eventually to hurt me and stop the spread of it. The people were there to guard me. I knew I was in good hands and didn't question their motives. At this point my parents were already on their way from Ontario, Canada, which was quite a trip considering they were instructed not to take a plane, since no airline would take a chance on me now.

That first night I woke up again of course, noticing that my disc-man was still with me on my bedside table. Everyone thought I was well asleep and I silently put it on for the first time in days and busted out in a rap by Ice Cube. I sang it loud and aggressively getting up from my bed, forwarding it onto my watchers. During this I got irritated at them looking at me and I felt that the messenger deserved some privacy. I pushed the dresser in front of the door to block them from coming and looking in. They eventually put it back and tried to calm me down. The girls' rooms were on this floor and I assumed I was keeping them up, but they would have been told to stay in because if I were to see them it would escalate the situation.

During the night when I was awake I would always here a ticking of a typewriter typing away every thought I had. For hours now I had sensed a very high-level Scientologist picking up my thoughts and transferring them onto paper to publish books in my name. Soon there would be many for the world.

Being close to the girl's rooms I felt a lot of support and I could feel their energy coming through the walls in waves of inspiration. I just had to survive this time in this room until the heat boiled over. Until it was safe to make my mark and bring the people the knowledge I had learned through my conscientious turmoil.

I had seen a nurse and a doctor on the grounds at some point. They too had to follow code. This meant nothing in terms of psychiatric drugs and no hospital. I had stopped eating for days and I don't remember them feeding me. I'm not saying they didn't though, I didn't want to eat and there was no making me do anything. I had lost 35 pounds in just over a week and I was thin to begin with. This didn't cross anyone's mind as an ambulance-worthy situation. This is what I don't get. This wasn't even a Scientology church (as if it would be excusable); instead, the people were recovering addicts. I don't know who these Scientology doctors are but they can't detect a critical situation and if they could they may not be aloud to do anything about it. It's a laughable joke that we need to take into direct action. I'm sure my death would've created more trouble for them then any Scientology ethics officer. My death wouldn't have been the first in Scientology hands. At the same time, if I ended up at some psych ward away from home, it wouldn't have been good for me. My parents could have lost me to the state for awhile. But this is not why an ambulance wasn't called for me. They just wanted me gone and my parents were driving thousands of miles scared shitless and the President of Scientology Canada calling off the hook, screaming to not let anyone give me lithium (a natural salt). Everyone was trying to help me apparently and their "help" was drawing me closer and closer to a cardiac arrest.

When I had to go to the washroom I was escorted. Sometimes I looked forward to the couple of minutes of social interaction. During the second day I was told I couldn't go to the washroom, at least not yet. So probably out of spite, I just started going in my pants. A counselor there was not pleased with me and that he had to clean it up. He was a nice guy and I had always liked him. Because I was starting to forget who he was, I laughed at his dismay. It was hard to distinguish from hour to hour whether

I thought they were there to help me or to take from me. From this idea I would lash out more. Two of them came at me with something, I thought a needle and for all I knew they were going to start stabbing me with it. So with a whimper I bent over and took it in the ass.

The needle calmed me down, but still couldn't produce a total comatose feeling or full sleep. From all of this what relaxed me were the mirages in the top left corner of my bedroom of Sting and Peter Gabriel and Phil Collins telling me to hang in there and that we were all waiting for you on the other side. Their smiles and praise coaxed me into a little sleep for a couple hours. It was not my mind that kept me restless anymore, but the detonation of each heart beat that would wake me after so long. Every second was beginning to feel like an imminent crisis and my body screaming for mercy.

As unsettling night turned to a desperate day what I remember was chaos. One of the counselors was trying to take me down for some reason and eventually was on top of my back, yelling for help because I was flinging him around and he couldn't take me down. Several more came to help and they tried to take me down. Whatever I was doing that started this problem I said that I would stop. "You might as well get off me because ten of you won't take me down, if I fought back you wouldn't be alive," I giggled. "I know you're just doing what you were told." I trailed off. I relaxed for a second then became frantic, stomping on a light bulb that was on the floor, smashing it into shooting fragments like my brain cells now, exploding and scattered. I was aware that I'd be leaving soon and felt that before I returned home all the people and all my enemies had to know that I meant well. Running into the exercise room there were screams from the top of my lungs; words of justification.

*" PLEASE LISTEN TO ME NOW. ALL OF
YOU"
" I AM COMING BACK TO MEET YOU
ALL" "PLEASE ACCEPT ME AND WHAT
I WILL BRING"
"I HAVE TO COME BACK AND SHOW
YOU WHAT I HAVE"
"PLEASE FORGIVE ME MY ENEMIES, I
FORGIVE
YOU AND WE ARE NO LONGER"
"I SWEAR TO GIVE ALL MY POWER IN
RETURN FOR A SAFE JOURNEY AND
PEACE WHEN I RETURN"*

This was my statement for the world: it was a vocal prayer to guarantee my survival on my journey home. I believed that the powerful mind readers of the world, top-Scientologists, psychics, spies for the FBI and all organizations, had their eyes on me now and could all hear this. This was my plea for my own safety. I walked out of the room breathless and passed the red head girl in the process. She was looking at me blankly and I raised my hand up for her to take it. She then pulled away and I gave her a knowing nod because I believed it was an act, a decoy. No one could know that we were to be together. It didn't matter to me because she would be taken back home by my people by the time I made it home. These ludicrous notions were starting to no longer build into theory, but form on a whim. Too fast, too crazy and blatant they were, now the pressure was on them to rush me out of here. They had no choice, but to wait in discomfort that didn't compare to mine.

A little later that evening one of the directors brought me out of the room to cool me off. We went in the main living room when everyone was out of the building. He told me to sit and relax and in doing that I got up after a minute and started circling him. I think he was trying to make things better, however I starting pacing and circling him like a bull or tiger ready to pounce. Then my anger would subside and I would unleash a tirade of accusations towards him and his conspirators, within this organization and elsewhere. This idea just came to me, and having this somewhat of a god-complex going I couldn't doubt myself. I went on to literally point fingers at him and I informed him that I knew of his escapades. I asked him why he felt the need to swindle money. I told him that I would be speaking with the real big wigs and an underground audit was coming his way. I started to smile, telling him that he wouldn't want that. I asked him if he would be confessing now. From my view he continued to play dumb. "You can't escape karma or my people," I finished by saying. I didn't get angry because my body could no longer tolerate the effort or stress, so right then my mind forgot that conversation literally by the time I walked out.

My parent's car rolled onto the burial ground at about nine at night. They were passed from one administrative building to another before they could see me. This was mostly to sign papers exempting them from any responsibility for my state. The head of administration said to my mother that she didn't tell him it could get this bad. My mother hadn't seen me yet, but she disagreed with him since she used the word psychotic when she was on the phone and describing what could happen with me. This word falls under ample warning because no matter how bad a person is acting it can't fall in a category worse than psychotic. I'm just not sure what his definition of the word was. It was fortunate that I wasn't a violent manic.

Next, they entered the building where I was being kept. They were in a hurry to finally get me help and yet an apprehension followed in having to see how bad my condition really was. I think that every parent believes in a reflection of themselves through their child, but this wasn't the best mirror image, although no one could be blamed directly.

I was brought out of hiding when they came. Seeing them I didn't say much right away, but they could tell by looking at me and by my pupils that it was as bad, probably worse than they had thought and feared. When I looked at them I wasn't overly happy or upset to see them, just exhausted. But I still had no desire for sleep. They were mostly unreal to me, hallucinations that I actually thought I was aware of this time. To them I was surreal; I had been in bad shape before, but with every passing moment they discovered that I paled in comparison to any son they knew. I snapped out of my delusion for a second, only to take on another delusion, thinking that my parents were only there for a briefing to give me some moral support through this mission I was on. I wasn't doing that well and I just needed their guidance, as they would soon be gone.

Before leaving, one of the young fellows was helping my parents pack my things and he too mentioned that the way they treated me wasn't right. Before he could elaborate someone again butted in, cutting communication by asking if there was a problem to save their own asses. To this day I'm not sure how I was treated in those few days or what happened overall. I have no idea what so ever what he meant by that. Maybe he just meant I should have been in a hospital or maybe something deeper. My door was then closed and we started driving away.

On the way out I cowered in my father's leather backseat, sure I was being escorted in luxury towards my death. I wasn't sure if my parents were trying to help me escape or regrettably taking me to my imminent execution. I was sure the others wouldn't let me escape knowing what I knew, the likes of which would ruin their operation. I started to whimper under my breath for my parents not to let them kill me. It looked as though we were going to a private sector of the grounds, which I thought would be quiet and sound proof. They kept driving and we passed the horses. I waived goodbye to them, deciding within a few seconds that I wasn't going to be killed, as we drove towards the road leading out of the facility. I didn't feel my danger had passed for good, but for the moment I let out a sigh and we were on our way home. The last week had felt like a grueling year to say the least.

ChapTer TwenTy-one

⁂

Driving east for a few hours it was time to get a motel. My parents were terrified for many reasons but for right now they just wanted me to sleep. I took a shower and came out looking in the mirror. I started to think now that I was Bruce Lee reincarnated as I flexed my body and started assaulting the air with punches and kicks. My mother assured me that I wasn't as she was grounding up more Atavin to put in my orange soda, the only thing I chose to ingest at this point for some reason. As the drugs were starting to kick in she relaxed me with a Scientology technique to relax the nerves. This massage put me out for the time being and a wave of relief came over them. My mother took a plastic tag tie off a luggage bag and put one end around my wrist and the other around hers as handcuffs, so she would feel me get up during the night. In case that didn't work, my father stacked chairs in front of the door to prevent a possible escape attempt. Before sleep they both prayed separately and differently just for me to sleep through the night for now. They knew to hope for a storybook ending was too far away to think about.

In the morning we were off as soon as possible. For the first time in a long time I had slept through the night and woke up a little tired because of the drugs. That drowsiness reminding me too much of being human and I didn't care for it. Miles into the abyss I was slipping in between different realities, all of them nonsensical but some much more rational than others. It was becoming increasingly clear to me that my parents were international alien spies who were using my parents' bodies for their safe travel. They were transporting me somewhere other than my destination and using mind powers to make me ignorant. I spent time having mind wars with them and usually felt I was close to finding out their plan. When losing the signal I would start to lose control and pretend I was going to jump out of the car, but my father screaming my name at me usually slugged me back into present time reality for a short period anyway.

We passed a large water tower in one city. The name across it was Lindsay the name of the ex-Vegas show girl from the detox centre. This was another excuse for symbolism that was telling me that they were watching over me and that I would be fine. Other times I believed my mother was the red-head girl I had liked. Not because she looked like her or I was hallucinating but because the alien spirit could morph any energy it felt fit to influence me their way. I started addressing my mother as Miriam at times. At other times it was because she was taking over my mother's body and it was the only way we could be together through astral exteriorization. This is a believed theory in Scientology that when the soul is on its own, out of the body, all it has to do is think and it can be anywhere due to thought travel. When there weren't any delusions, for short periods of time my mother was just mom. I'd act like a kid and ask for things and giggle or try to peer into her soul through intense eye contact, with a look that said you are the reason I am like this.

My mother was now sitting beside me in the car to talk to me and settle me down. It didn't last long because my behavior had become more erratic and frantic. My father ended up beside me to physically restrain me when I started to attempt to jump out of the car into the highway for real. I was becoming scared and desperate. He would put the seat belt back on me and I would know it was daddy and a few minutes later I would forget and take it back off to escape whoever he really was. The claustrophobic feeling was more than I could bear, along with the other feelings of unfamiliarity. When I did get out of the car to go to the bathroom I would jump around and do cartwheels in joy, happy to get out. I could only drink liquids and I developed an overactive bladder from physical stress.

During restroom breaks from state to state I started putting fear in urinating men across America. I would bring up uncomfortable topics, ask personal questions to men pissing, and physically intimidate some of them. Even big bikers would try to get away from me quickly. I was fucked, as my mother so eloquently, but so accurately put it. At truck stops I would watch all the fat truckers walking with their arms out as if it was muscle, their fat arms hanging off a back drop of back fat. I would walk by all of them imitating their walk as my father gave them a look of apology and tried to get me to stop out of fear. I looked at my father and told him not to apologize for me because I was not his slave, in fact I had created him.

My father got to the point where he didn't want to take me anywhere anymore. He was afraid for his life. He just as soon let me go wherever I wanted away from the public. My parents' general fear was starting to waver from panic to exhaustion and then back to panic. Hope is something that always has to be there to get through a situation. They stayed strong, but when your first born is a flat out crazy person and no one seems to know what to do, who do you rely on? They both had different ideas of what was going to happen to me when we got back home and the real fear was me not getting back. Potentially spending the rest of my life in some U.S. insane asylum where people never come back in any sense of the phrase.

The second night we found another motel somewhere. I don't remember anything and my parents happen to not either. I assume things weren't very good because the brain's defense mechanism doesn't filter out good events. My parents had to worry about even getting a motel room. If anyone had seen me I would have been deemed a liability and a risk. I stayed in the car, while my father registered for the night and my mother tried to reason with me and bring some sense of reality back, trying to impress on me the meaning and consequences of my actions. My father returned to the car and stated what he needed from me. I took the proposals like a business agreement and listened. I have no way of knowing what transpired, but we were able to get through the night.

What we had ahead of us was the last mile home so to speak. Early on, I started to address my father as L Ron Hubbard, since I was his reincarnated son. This was a step up perhaps, because I was acknowledging again that he was my father in a sense. He continued to have to stay in the back with me for the rest of the stretch that would be the ending of what seemed like an eternity. All of the sudden, the border approached quickly. My parents were trying to calm me down knowing well there wasn't much they could do this time. I was starting to develop olfactory hallucinations. The smell was unbearable, I can't describe it, but the rot was unearthly. They had to get me back home and prolonging the situation was only going to make me worse.

Driving ahead they would speak to me hoping a word or phrase would sink in so I could grasp what was really going on. They bickered back and forth telling each other what they were going to do, telling each other it would be ok and then not being sure. Inside, they were both terrified. My mother prayed to whatever it was that could help us. I had some fast food not long before and a beyond rotten smell that didn't exist was making me sick. Coming up to the border gates vomit spewed all over my father's shoes. He yelled to my mom asking her what he should do. She just told him to let me puke. My mother saw this as her prayer answered. When the guard asked what was wrong with her son, she said that I had been physically ill and I just sat there normal, partly recovering from the heave. We were let through.

A sigh of relief was let out of the open windows. I said out loud, "I knew it," as if I had controlled her mind to let us by. I gave one of my gestures with my hands to signal acknowledgment of knowingness to myself. The ease of tension was momentary again but a huge gain. I stared at all the cars around us and I thought these were all authorities waiting to escort us the rest of the way home. I giggled to see my entourage finally, as I called it. I would be respected soon in my home country for what I brought back and shortly the world would be able to benefit.

Home was still a couple hours away. Almost immediately after leaving the border, in the comfort of knowing I was safe, I lost it again. Thoughts weren't able to stick for more than a few seconds anymore. My father cleaned the puke off his shoes and we bolted for home. My head was starting to spin from my thoughts. I had to be strong to make it home, but my mind re-routed into thinking this wasn't what was best. And had I forgotten so soon – were they spies? Where were they really taking me? I didn't recognize any of this. For all I knew we could be anywhere. There were people who wanted me dead and I couldn't trust anyone anymore. Even if they were my parents, I wasn't sure to trust them anymore. When we got home my father had Scientologists that were going to care for me out of only respect to him, and my mother was going to crash the car into a hospital emergency entrance.

Twenty minutes from home we stopped because I told my parents I needed to pee. Before exiting I asked my mother where we were. I recognized the name of the town. I asked, "This is where I was born mom, isn't it?"

"Yes, that's right," she responded.

"Well mom, you know you brought me into this world and you can take me out."

I went to bolt out of the car to run. My father swung around to my side to stop me. I didn't know who he was anymore. I picked him up off the ground like he was a child and threw him against the truck. I had lost at least thirty pounds, but my brain's delusion had given my body momentum and strength. He slid down the truck to his knees. I then stepped onto the express route and stood there. A transport truck was coming my way. My arm raised and I put my hand out knowing I could stop it with my mind. My parents started screaming, the high pitch terror jolting me back onto the side. I went onto the grass and did a cartwheel and started to walk away, the idea of what I had done starting to affect me, not fully knowing if it was right or wrong. He started to plead and beg for me to come home. He told me that everything was waiting for me and that there were plenty of nice things. I took this as a bribe and I told my father, spirits can't be bought, and he should know that.

I tore through a nearby mechanic shop, panting and pacing. The old Canadian farmers aren't much for gawking and gossiping and they let me be for awhile. My parents came through, and soon after they called 911. I sat down in a chair. One of the good old boys said, "Hey boy, you're looking a little thin," and he offered me a banana. I sucked it down in a second, my body moaning for nutrients, not being able to notice until the first bite. I got up immediately as if I were energized from it and started moving around like a boxer punching the showcase tires and rambling incoherently.

By the time the cops arrived I was on the ground sobbing. They stood over me in their authoritative positions asking my parents if I wanted to press charges and asking if I was on drugs then pressing the question again in disbelief that I wasn't. Cops like to deal with everything and understand nothing. The ambulance arrived as I was starting to get aggravated from the police hovering over me like ignorant waste. The ambulance driver got down on his hands and knees and talked to me as if I were still a person.

"Hi son, whats going on?"

I looked up in pain and said, "Thoughts, thoughts, too many thoughts!" finally defeated.

"Why don't you come with me, we're gonna get you something to rest and slow down these thoughts ok?"

"Ya, yes I think I need that," I cried.

I was taken to the ambulance by him and covered by a blanket. There were a few other paramedics there. The man asked me what my name, age and address was to verify where I was. I responded in a quick and orderly fashion like a marine and then blacked out. As the ambulance skidded out of the dirt parking lot my father stood and allowed himself to cry for the first time since maybe the suicide attempt a couple years earlier. Fearful and unknowing what would happen to his first-born and most likely dumbfounded in how he created a son that was a living example of a contradiction to his faith.

We can dream, maybe conceive
A perfect reflection,
Of a life without rejection.
No troubles or pain. But where is the gain?
Turmoil makes us question, Makes us scream
out our confession.
A dream is unattainable without struggle.
Even a life story without this lesson Deserves
a muzzle.

ChapTer TwenTy-Two

The emergency doors opened and I came to, as I was being hauled in on the stretcher. They couldn't have a crazy person out in general admittance flailing around. Soon after I was let out, because I ended up in a waiting room alone with two cops guarding the door. This only fed my delusions of grandeur. They were hiding and guarding me from the fans and the assassins. I kept telling them to keep on guard because the swarm was coming. I kept drinking little Dixie cups of water then crushing them in my hand and kung-fu kicking them across the room. My energy had some how replenished itself once again. The cops were ignoring me and I didn't like it. I asked them if they knew who I was. On the door was a blurry window and between their backs was a book stand. I started to see books that had been written by me and I told the cops to pick them up. When this didn't work I started to push the door in on them.

Soon after, I was coaxed into the stretcher again because they had a room ready for me in the psychiatric ward. One of the cops was present and when I wasn't looking he strapped my arm in before I could fight back. I gave him a filthy look as if he were my executioner. I looked at my mom to my other side pleading because I was sure, this was it. I asked her how she could do this to me. As I was being wheeled off I felt the prick of a needle with a heavy shot. I noticed the effects right away and felt myself slipping away into what I thought was the end of this life. I convinced myself that the only way the Government could deal with me was to put me down. As the sedative started to sink in I was thankful it was such a peaceful death.

I woke up in darkness on a mattress in hospital clothes and started crawling around to scope out my new environment. I didn't know how long I would be there for so I might have to adapt. All there was to learn was a bathroom to my right that wouldn't open and a window that wouldn't either, or give any light. The door in front of me again had a blurry out-look. I saw outlines and shadows, but couldn't make out anything. I gave it a knock, but nobody would come. So I felt forced to take a shit, cowering in the corner and then I took a piss in the other. I watched a nurse come in quickly and clean it up. She wouldn't make eye contact with me so nothing was said. I had no idea how she knew of my mess. I thought they must have had special cameras watching, trying to steal my ideas and thoughts. Even the hospital has to adhere to the officials. When she left I heard a buzzing come from the bathroom. I slowly crawled up to it, tapping it like a caveman. It was open now. I went inside to check out the view, took off my shirt and propped it in between the door and the wall to avoid that mishap again and left. On the other side of the bathroom was another door. After a few minutes, the bathroom door opened and a hand threw my shirt back in the room, scaring the shit out of me. Where did she come from? Who were these people? How do they know my every move? I'd have to be much more careful.

I paced again in continued solitude. Somehow, I was getting better, subconsciously knowing maybe that I was safe now. I tried looking out the window that was made of unbreakable plastic, which had a curtain on the inside. The curtain was pushed to the side just enough that I could see people coming in off the street with flowers and gifts. Again, I thought that they were for me and that my humanitarian work was by now getting to the public. That thought kept me patient until I was transferred.

ChapTer TwenTy-Three

I was taken closer to home to be more closely watched by my family and my psychiatrist. The hospital put me on a form 1. This is given to patients who are a liability and cannot be discharged until they are better. I started off with a lock down room of course right away where there was a mattress on the floor. The bathroom was mostly locked because patients try to hurt themselves or vandalize it. I wasn't in the emotional state to do that, but kept having to go to the bathroom on the floor. The nurse that was supposed to be looking after me wasn't. After days of cleaning up after me, my mother went to the nurse's station and screamed. She was a head nurse at this hospital and wasn't taking any shit from lazy women that probably thought I was trash too.

My treatment shaped up immediately. Not that I noticed. They were still trying to get me to sleep. For weeks they had me on anything short of horse tranquilizers even though the dosages would have killed a couple by now. I still would not and could not sleep much. I still considered sleep a punishment. My delusional motivation could have kept me going until my heart stopped and it came close. On top of having to deal with her son being a fucking loon now, my mother was still being bombarded by Scientologist's phone calls telling her not to let me take these drugs or those drugs. They were also yelling at her and abusing my mother on the phone, telling her what a mistake it was and what a mistake I was in so many words. My mother forwarded them to the Scientologist doctor that we had seen before. It took her telling them that I was past these trivial Scientology remedies and needed the "big guns" now for them to lay off. I guess it takes nothing short of a high level Scientologist with a medical

P.H.D to get anything. Once I actually got some sleep, I was allowed to integrate with the general public a little bit. It would usually excite me too much and would be forcefully sent back down to my holding cell. I would spend countless hours wailing away at the door, punching and kicking until I tired myself out a little with the help of meds. Once and awhile I went up to the door and started banging again only to realize it was open and probably had been for awhile. This didn't please me because I had figured it was my "furious thunder" that loosened the lock. The nerve they had, locking the door on me in the first place. My anger for that would come out and I would be placed back in there, sometimes easily and sometimes with more difficulty. I usually listened to the nurses because some of them were friends of the family, and deep down knew they meant well. I still couldn't control my mouth however. Sometimes security was called to come down with a sedative. Strange things would happen on full moon nights. Behaviors would escalate not only with myself but with others as anyone who works in this field can tell you. The moon seems to set people up for some sort of astrological metamorphosis.

One day I just started running. My effort made me feel like I was going fast, but my legs weren't actually in quick rotation. I could hardly see in front of me, looking down my feet meshed with the ground, being drugged up so heavily. I stopped just outside the gate because I knew the guard was going to catch me. My sight was a blur like most of my life lately. It wasn't a secure fortress by any means. Early on, I ran out in mid-traffic to cross the street. There was an anti-abortion picket. I ran over and started yelling, "Power to the people!" I came back because the nurse was pleading with me and told me he would lose his job. I liked him and ran back.

When I was spending time with the Sea Org people, there was a girl that used to come around the church. Her mother was old- time Scientology friends with my parents. We spent time together during this time and I also developed a crush on her. When I was out in the court yard she came to visit me one day. We spent time sitting in the grass talking. The medication was still making me drool a little, even though I tried to be serious with her. We talked for awhile and I asked her if when I get out we could be boyfriend and girlfriend, being past innuendos. She told me that we could talk about that when I got out of here and that was fine with me. I never saw her again. It seemed to make sense that we could be together but luck would still be non-existent, romantically or any other way.

I still had in my possession my disc-man and my music. Barking and growling echoed from my four walls and in the halls. The nurses informed my mother one day that they thought we might have a problem, which would be Turrets Syndrome. My mother laughed and said that was just 'his damn DMX music.' She told them that it needed to be taken away from me.

The only problem was that I had Bipolar Disorder and it had been deemed at a type 1, which of course is the more serious kind, judging from this story. My personality at the time was being fueled by religious fanaticism and a refusal to sleep made it a more serious case. It was already accepted that I would be on medication the rest of my life and that was ok, just as long as I got better. There are quite a few different types of the disorder and they are all individual. A type 3 can act worse than a type 1, it all depends on who does or doesn't get help or meds or whose personality elevates or depreciates the event with conflicting factors. A person who was once crazy can be more productive than anyone around them eventually with help; conversely, people who choose to haphazardly take their meds can be a little off the rest of their life and get nothing done, but appear normal. This is why we can't generalize anything and say what's good for everyone or anyone until we know going on individually.

At this point, of course, it wasn't that much of a surprise that I had a diagnosable mental illness as it was a relief. It seems easy to diagnose it from the outside but that's when medication gets prescribed needlessly and harmfully. I had to cycle at least twice full-circle from severe depression to extreme mania to be given the Bipolar type 1 label. Scientology was my choice. All my parents wanted was my sanity and to be back to normal. They had no disappointment in me because they had never pushed it on me and they had doubts that I would ever be interested in Scientology if I was acting like myself. All they had left to be disappointed in was Scientology after the time, money and effort they put into it, just its people denied and had pity for their son.

ChapTer TwenTy-four

→

When I would get out of what had become my permanent holding room, people in worse condition would sometimes get a hold of me. They talked in riddles and symbolism and everything meant something. I was right there with them until they were taken away for making me over-excited. One night upon being let into the general public bed, a crazy lady jumped in bed with me and initiated contact. She kissed me and without any recourse on my part, she asked if that was it? I responded with a "yes" in horror. There were times like the one where I was talking with a young guy telling him that I knew his response because I created his thought. He punched me in the face. I had forgotten it happened, or not even realized by the time he walked away. When he was in the nurse's station, upset and confessing I was long into another thought, not aware it ever happened.

I began to be friends with a girl. We spent time together and eventually ended up in one of the uncomfortable lounge couches making out. I had forgotten what it was like to interact with people especially romantically even though I was still unusually doped up. I looked at her and told her that I was so hard right now. I think it came as a surprise since I had forgotten about that area of specialty for quite some time. She didn't laugh at me however, and I dragged her in my room that was nearby. We were touching and she kept saying that we were going to get caught. At first it didn't register totally and I didn't really care. I didn't have much to lose, but my virginity. All of a sudden something dawned on me. I suppose the fear of getting caught, though nothing would've happened to me. I then threw her out of the room. She was just standing there for awhile as if to say she didn't really want to stop. I closed the door on her and pulled down my pants to relieve months of tension. How many chances for manhood could I foil here?

It wasn't long before she was let out and I was left behind. Finally, after months in there I received my own steady room and my own clothes back. I don't think I wanted to leave, I just needed a walk. I put on my Air Jordan's and my hat and kept my hospital clothes on since I was so used to them. I also put on a pair of sunglasses I had and walked right out. It must have been in between an early morning shift change because no one noticed. I had already forgotten that I wasn't allowed to leave so I left very casually, which was also a contributor to my inconspicuousness.

I walked outside beyond the gate and onto the street. I wanted to go downtown like before. Maybe I wanted to get a sense of freedom back. My footsteps kept on and I didn't look back and no one followed. The outside world and my town seemed so foreign now, though nothing had changed, with each step it became more familiar like I had never left. It was as though I had come from the womb again and each passing second it became that much easier to breathe. As I was still heavily sedated, the blur was affecting me, but the exhilaration of feeling on my own again kept me looking ahead and light on my feet. In almost no time, I was in the downtown core.

The Scientology doors were locked. It was too early and they hadn't opened yet. I was going to visit and started to get upset. In the alleyway beside the building were some Catholic

School kids huddled together laughing and talking. I looked at them and pointed out the black kid of the group. I said, "Yo" to get his attention. He looked at me and I asked him if he rapped, somewhat prejudiced. He said that he did, coincidentally. I then pulled out a C.D. jacket I had in a plastic bag I was carrying. I told him that we had to start a group now and rap at this concert. He pulled back kind of shocked as he joined his friends to stare, and before I could press on, I noticed some kids were yelling at me from across the street. I ended my conversation, as I was distracted by two young boys who said not to fuck with them, as I walked over to them aggressively. They said they belonged to gangs, but I took a walk with them anyway. They asked to borrow my disc man which was also in the bag. They said they were going to take a walk and meet me back here. I was under the impression that I could teleport messages onto C.D's. I let them borrow it because they needed to learn the negative outcomes of being involved in gangs that were highlighted in my messages I had just created. I then left with the intention to come back, but never did, because my attention span and memory had disappeared for months now. It was safe to assume they didn't come back either.

Making my way back up around the block I had forgotten already about the young thugs who I gave a chance to steal. I walked into a downtown mall where I suddenly remembered that I used to enjoy a medium French vanilla coffee there. I walked to the counter and ordered my previous to now usual.

When the Asian man delivered the cost I looked at him funny because I had forgotten about the use of money in this world. I looked beside me and up, way up to a "6, 9" Kenyan man, then back at the Asian owner. I told him that the tall man would pay for it, since I was sure he knew who I was. I then walked away. I guess they shrugged it off, most likely noticing my hospital garb. Why start a crazy riot over a dollar? Or possibly the man treated me.

I had walked right up to another man and sat with him without asking. I was very intense, shooting off about unjustly actions of the world and how we need to change the school system. He held his ground however, and kept at least the demeanor of being comfortable. We sat and talked and he let me get out whatever ranting I felt I had to. I cannot recall any time between this point and when I stepped into a black SUV of some kind. This man somehow kept me calm and got me back to the hospital without a fight. My mom told me that a man called the house, telling them that I was safe and that he was taking me back. She asked his name and he told her that it wasn't important. I'm not sure how he got my number either. I'm not sure I was in the state of remembering if he did ask. I arrived back at the hospital and he disappeared. It seemed as though he was an angel or sent by one.

Getting back, there were some cops around. I sat in a cop car for a bit until it was safe to transfer me back down. I was flaunting with my sunglasses on, trying to show off for the paparazzi's eye that was on me. I was pretty sure the cops would handle them. The only one in fact watching me was my high school counselor. She had an appointment that day at the hospital and she could see me through the windows. At our last meeting I was a suicidal kid who had such promise at one point, and now I was a raving lunatic that couldn't be stopped. She didn't know how this could happen to someone, especially one of her own students. She broke down and cried right there.

After being put in the pit for a few days to calm down, things started to get better. I looked forward to my first movie night and watched George of the Jungle, and besides freaking out because I was wearing the same Nike's as Brendan Fraser in the movie, the isolations stopped. I lived the next month in a normal patient room. I started to write poetry, though my vision made it difficult. I began to gather rational, coherent thoughts again and I started to make friends. My weight was coming back to normal, the meds slowing down my manic metabolism. I was now in a state where people could visit with me more often. Soon after having my 19th birthday party in a psychiatric ward, all too soon it was finally time to go. The storm had passed and reality started to come back into play for better and worse. I realized partially that what had happened was only because of medication and rest. I also began to be more like myself whatever that was. As a teenager we're all a little confused, I was more than most with the imbalance. When I got into the car to go home I wasn't sure still if it was for good. Maybe part of me was scared to leave, as many ill people depend on the system to bail them out of responsibility for their entire life. I didn't think I wanted to return, but anything can become comfortable after time. The five minute drive home seemed a world away to me now. Soon after the hospital fence would be made to stand solid and ten feet high.

It would be a few years still until my brain fully recovered and I could or would think logically as to what transpired. A lot of my views in this book did and still do go against the systems flaws but if it wasn't for my system, my government and my psychiatrist in this predicament there would be nothing to write about. I was trained at one time to see all psychiatrists as sinister; if it wasn't for mine who was trained to and only wanted to help people, I can assure you that I would be dead.

afTerworD

Mental illness doesn't have to be a sentence. People shouldn't be judged for it, because anyone who doesn't find a cure for their afflictions belongs to a permanent mind prison. Most illness can be regulated, if not fully controlled. Some people with Bipolar Disorder choose not to take their medication because of the 'high' they get from the disorder; it becomes like any high, and becomes an addiction. Either that or the illness causes a block in distinguishing between healthy good moods and mania. The fact that people fall again and again by not consistently taking the medication is an indication that a change has to be made. It is also because of lack of support that people are forced out of the potential to live a regular life and into a void of obscurity.

People will tell you, and it has been written, that bipolar or mentally ill people in general are bound to fail. That we cannot keep relationships or hold down jobs or be successful. This of course is very true of an ill person, in fact any person failing in life could be deemed mentally ill, since they are not showcasing the mental skills and tools to live properly. Diagnosed or not, it is fair to say that any brain not in contact with the environment is ill. The distinguishment between sick and healthy isn't stated clearly. The generality of mentioning everybody is the myth.

My life since recovery has been very normal, if not painfully normal from a bipolar person's point of view. This took time, introspection and countless hours of self-reflection to achieve. However, being stable is the most important thing.

A person living any life is always shown a light to salvation. They just have to choose and follow that inner guide or sometimes seek an outside sign to find redemption. I am led to believe and have to, that we are all given chances to turn situations around and ultimately our lives if we want to. Only when we want to does the chance present itself. Illness, like anything this world can offer, could be nothing more than a setback. We all need to overcome our hurdles in this life. There is no need to make more by drowning in a present situation. Mental illness is no more severe than any other human flaw and to pity us or to belittle us is an insult to someone with most likely a lot of potential behind that wall of mental blockage. It's not that we don't have fully functioning brains, it's that they are over active and sometimes over functioning; this leads to an overload and then to temporary irrationality.

From my perspective, mental illness is defined as any abnormal or imbalanced brain activity that leads to inappropriate actions, this being enough for diagnosis and sometimes too soon a course for medication. For any particular disease to be scrutinized is ludicrous. ADHD is widely accepted now as a mental illness, whether it is always legitimate or a 'pawned off ' explanation for something else. Whether one is overtaken by the lies of whatever religion in which they are immersed, or if they have a valid mental illness, or if someone was abused by their father as a child -- it all comes down to the same thing. This behaviour is a potential link toward irrationality, which can be just as dangerous if not the same or worse than mental illness. We can not escape what runs through our path, but everyone is responsible to carry on walking through individual notion and effort.

People judge mental illness through hearsay or the severity of the affects, however mental illness is only as dangerous as the individual behind the wheel. Many of the most dangerous people in the world didn't have anything wrong with their brains, just a problem with their minds, thoughts, lives and maybe spirits. They were of course mentally ill, so to speak, only in a worse definition. This was their natural design or something that cannot be easily rehabilitated. It is natural to be ill and insane in the kind of world we occupy. Anyone able to realize dysfunction and seek help is the closest to sanity most might ever achieve. We are all afflicted and some of us will always be. Mental illness could never stop the power of a person's will to be good and could never get in the way of a person's ulterior sickness for ill intent. In few cases do legitimate illnesses make people do unspeakable things which are unlike themselves. This only happens with ignorance, lack of education and support. Being diagnosed does not make me any more sick then the millions out there who deny, regress, and avoid, etc. their own problems are no less ill pretending that they are fine.

In this respect, to put "diagnosed" people in a box seems unfair. Some of us need drugs to make us better. This is accepted, but not always believed by people, which hurts and makes our lives a lie. Some people get mentally ill by taking drugs and this seems to be socially accepted. From what I've seen and judging by my own experience, there is no reason why a bipolar person cannot lead a productive life. People's emotional and social flaws and fears disappear on the high. An addict on drugs is the same as a bipolar person off drugs in terms of emotion. The cure being the same and different in that the bipolar must learn to live on drugs since it's not convenient and there's no psychotropic trip to it and the addict has to learn to live off drugs to break the dependency. This could affiliate with many social dilemmas. It's all about people finding themselves and finding a reason to have a natural healthy high.

To have a brain is to be susceptible to emotional turmoil, past memories, any kind of trauma, stress, and genetic predisposition and so on. There are vast amounts of things in life that can change brain chemistry. No one is really safe from flying off the handle and everyone has the ability to be feared because everyone is an individual within an inconstant field. No matter how sick someone is, a natural innate consciousness is still speaking to them inside on some level. In the end, we can rest assure, it will usually come through and there is help in this god-forsaken world for them.

Scientologists will tell that you I went crazy because of a few anti-depressants or because I am a lost cause. Even though I have been taking medication ever since and I am fine now. Types of naturopaths will say that my symptoms were due to stress. Neurologists said there was nothing wrong except me and my behavior because they didn't test for the right illness. Some say disease is mental, but no one chooses to go psychotic. Psychiatrists will say I'm bipolar type 1 and I have to trust this because under their care I became better under supervision and medication and my symptoms matched the book to a tee. There are some bipolar people that can get by without medication, many do and not all cases are as black and white as mine. Most people's inherent underlying personalities wouldn't take the illness to such extremes as I did, but it can happen with a type

1. It was arduous to go through this just to become diagnosed, but that is each person's individual journey, like life and the progression of self. To generalize people in boxes is to encapsulate their souls with this view. I would much rather go through this than a life time of struggling with the direct afflictions of an imbalance taking affect daily and maybe that's why it did.

I know religion was created for a reason. I know what the right reason would be. I'm not sure that was ever the main intention. I still support anything that brings more hope into a life that cannot find it through ability. If anything makes life more livable for someone then by all means endorse it. We join religions for different reasons, some good some bad. I probably wouldn't have joined Scientology if I wasn't sick, but I'm still searching for the same answers. No one should be judged because they have no belief, since they might already have enough hope to live happily and the scrutiny is really just jealousy.

I have been told by a Scientologist that they accept my illness now. Apparently they read more data on it. Yet, this seems like a ploy to get my family back into the church. Despite all of this, they are still saying that they can get me off medication, even after seeing how well I'm doing. How contradictory, as if they haven't caused us enough grief. What nerve these people have to do this. They literally won't be satisfied until I'm dead and that's before this book. Scientology does state that medication is not needed. But they don't always mention and sometimes forget that this advice pertains to a healthy mind. Maybe disease cannot live in a healthy mind, but how many minds are born flawless? Until everyone is free of disease, (which even most Scientologists can't verify of themselves), there will always be medication. Medication is here to make money and it works. Scientology is here to make money and some of the data is true but should cost nothing, since the information is all around us for free if we look. Scientology isn't just dangerous for someone who needs medication; its direct purpose is something other than what the members are aware of. You could give a placebo pill to someone with an affliction and they might get better, which proves they were being fooled in the first place. Like Scientology, this is an empty promise that shows no results, just the illusion of them. I'll stick with the real pills because the results have lead to a distinguishable proven result.

Hubbard stated many times that once one reaches that state of Clear a person will cease to have irrational, emotional and physical ills. My mother having attained the "state" has been suffering of Multiple Sclerosis for years now. Scientologists get sick all the time especially due to the high demands and stress. Ironically since getting therapeutic on Lithium I haven't had so much as a common cold in 6 years. Medical doctors account for the strengthening of the immune system after prolonged use. My parents are no longer Scientologists. The ordeal made them see a little more clearly to say the least.

If I have learned anything, it is that freedom and a higher knowledge of any kind shouldn't cost anything more than the time and effort you put forth in finding it. It cannot be gained through ignorance: seek and you shall find a higher truth for you. Truth must be found by you and register practically in your life and must not be ever stated for you by another.